MORE PRAISE FOR

Dave Barry's History of the Millennium (So Far)

"The latest book by Pulitzer Prize–winning humorist Dave Barry is his twisted take on the first few years of the new millennium, prefaced by his equally warped overview of the previous 1,000 years. . . . There's nothing harder for a writer than to be consistently funny but Barry always makes it look ridiculously easy. He seamlessly segues from his glib twists on news stories to taking jabs at political figures to offering up general mockery. . . . His fans already know what to expect: one or two chuckles per paragraph, a guffaw every page or two, and tear-inducing laughter a couple of times each chapter."
—The Associated Press

"[A] very funny guy."
—*Sacramento Bee*

"Barry's irreverent view of recent history . . . consists of month-to-month commentary on the most outrageous events of the year . . . all delivered with Barry's hilarious look at the absurdities of American life. . . . Barry fans and readers looking for a lighter perspective on the history of world events will enjoy this book."
—*Booklist*

"[An] uproarious recap of a bunch of history we wish we could forget."
—*St. Petersburg Times*

"Barry is up to hoary old tricks: non sequiturs, running gags, mishmashed metaphors. This is history willy-nilly, and, unusual for Barry, it's entirely booger-free. A book that's fearless in the face of fact."
—*Kirkus Reviews*

ALSO BY DAVE BARRY

FICTION

The Shepherd, the Angel, and Walter the Christmas Miracle Dog

Cave of the Dark Wind (with Ridley Pearson)

Escape from the Carnivale (with Ridley Pearson)

Peter and the Shadow Thieves (with Ridley Pearson)

Peter and the Starcatchers (with Ridley Pearson)

Tricky Business

Big Trouble

NONFICTION

Dave Barry's Money Secrets

Boogers Are My Beat

Dave Barry Hits Below the Beltway

Dave Barry Is Not Taking This Sitting Down

Dave Barry Turns 50

Dave Barry Is from Mars and Venus

Dave Barry's Book of Bad Songs

Dave Barry in Cyberspace

Dave Barry's Complete Guide to Guys

Dave Barry's Gift Guide to End All Gift Guides

Dave Barry Is NOT Making This Up

Dave Barry Does Japan

Dave Barry's Only Travel Guide You'll Ever Need

Dave Barry Talks Back

Dave Barry Turns 40

Dave Barry Slept Here

Dave Barry's Greatest Hits

Homes and Other Black Holes

Dave Barry's Guide to Marriage and/or Sex

Dave Barry's Bad Habits

Claw Your Way to the Top

Stay Fit and Healthy Until You're Dead

Babies and Other Hazards of Sex

The Taming of the Screw

Dave Barry

BERKLEY BOOKS

New York

DAVE BARRY'S

HISTORY

of the

MILLENNIUM

(so far)

THE BERKLEY PUBLISHING GROUP
Published by the Penguin Group
Penguin Group (USA) Inc.
375 Hudson Street, New York, New York 10014, USA
Penguin Group (Canada), 90 Eglinton Avenue East, Suite 700, Toronto, Ontario M4P 2Y3, Canada
(a division of Pearson Penguin Canada Inc.)
Penguin Books Ltd, 80 Strand, London WC2R 0RL, England
Penguin Ireland, 25 St. Stephen's Green, Dublin 2, Ireland (a division of Penguin Books Ltd.)
Penguin Group (Australia), 250 Camberwell Road, Camberwell, Victoria 3124, Australia
(a division of Pearson Australia Group Pty. Ltd.)
Penguin Books India Pvt. Ltd., 11 Community Centre, Panchsheel Park, New Delhi—110 017, India
Penguin Group (NZ), 67 Apollo Drive, Rosedale, North Shore 0632, New Zealand
(a division of Pearson New Zealand Ltd.)
Penguin Books (South Africa) (Pty.) Ltd., 24 Sturdee Avenue, Rosebank, Johannesburg 2196,
South Africa

Penguin Books Ltd, Registered Offices: 80 Strand, London WC2R 0RL, England

The publisher does not have any control over and does not assume any responsibility for author
or third-party websites or their content.

Selections from this book first appeared in *The Miami Herald*.

PRINTING HISTORY
G. P. Putnam's Sons hardcover edition / September 2008
Berkley trade paperback edition / August 2008

Berkley trade paperback ISBN: 978-0-425-22165-5

The Library of Congress has cataloged the G. P. Putnam's Sons hardcover edition as follows:

Barry, Dave.
Dave Barry's history of the millennium (so far) / Dave Barry.
p.   cm.
ISBN 978-0-399-15437-9
1. History—Humor.   2. History—21st century—Humor.
3. American wit and humor.   I. Title.
PN6231.H47B37   2007   2007014131
818'.5402—dc22

PRINTED IN THE UNITED STATES OF AMERICA

10   9   8   7   6   5   4   3   2   1

DAVE BARRY'S
HISTORY
of the
MILLENNIUM
(so far)

FOREWORD

As Abraham Lincoln once said, "Journalism is the first rough draft of history."

Or possibly it was Thomas Edison who said that. I'm pretty sure *somebody* said it, because you often hear journalists quote it in an effort to explain how come they get everything wrong.

We see this all the time. Journalists, rushing to get a story out under deadline pressure, will report—based on preliminary information—that a ship sank, and 127 people, many of them elderly, perished. Then, upon further investigation, it turns out that nobody, in fact, perished, although one elderly person was slightly injured by a set of dentures hurled by another elderly person in an effort to get the first elderly person to stop talking so loud. Then it turns out that this happened at a nursing home, as opposed to a ship, although the elderly people *were* watching a video of *Titanic* at the time, and although there were only four of them, as opposed to 127, the nursing home *is* located on Route 124, which is only three less than 127, which is not that much of an error when you consider the deadline pressure that journalists operate under.

That's what we journalists mean when we talk about "the first rough draft of history."

I was a practicing journalist for a number of years.[1] I started in 1971 as a cub reporter at the *Daily Local News* in West Chester, Pa., and I can honestly say that at least 87 percent of the time when I produced a news story I had no idea what the hell I was talking about. For example, one of the beats I was assigned to cover was the Downingtown Area Regional Sewer Authority, which, as you might imagine, was an authority responsible for the regional sewage of the Downingtown area. I was an English major. I had learned, in college, to explain the difference between the metaphysical and Cavalier styles of British poetry.[2] I had learned nothing about wastewater treatment, a topic rarely addressed in seventeenth-century British literature.

Yet there I was, wearing a sport coat and taking notes in my official reporter notebook, as the members of the

---

[1] One hundred twenty-seven years, to be exact.
[2] The difference is, they are both boring.

Downingtown Area Regional Sewer Authority discussed, at *great* length, matters pertaining to sewage, such as "sewer interceptors." The Authority was always talking about these, and I wrote many long stories about them, but to this day I have no idea what they are or why anybody would *want* to intercept sewage. I'm sure that the stories I wrote made no sense; fortunately, as far as I could tell, nobody was reading them.

I spent several years cranking out the first rough draft of Downingtown-area sewage history before moving on to other areas of journalism. Eventually, I became a columnist, which is the branch of journalism where instead of attempting to explain topics that you don't know anything about you have strong opinions about them. Some columnists are really good at this. You can wake them up from a dead sleep and ask them: "Should the UN send troops to East Zambora?" Or: "Should the San Francisco city council ban nitrogen from the atmosphere?" Or: "Which is a better style of British poetry, the metaphysical or the Cavalier?" And these columnists will instantly feel very strongly one way or another, and produce six hundred passionate words in support of their views. They can do this *even though there is no such place as East Zambora*. That is the opinion-generating power that your true columnist possesses.

Me, I can't do it. There are very few issues[3] about which I have strong opinions; beyond those, I generally don't get riled

---

[3] Beer; low-flow toilets; Donald Trump's hair; and beer.

up. So I have spent my columnizing career writing mostly about "offbeat" topics such as the alarming decline of American capabilities in the field of accordion repair, or the man who came up with the idea—which I am not making up—of keeping turkey rectums shut with Super Glue.[4] This kind of story is my bread and butter; I let the other columnists deal with the hard news.

The exception is the "Year in Review." This is my one effort to participate, as a journalist, in the writing of the first rough draft of history. Each year, along about Halloween, I start going through the headlines, month by month, summarizing the big stories that happened during that year. My deadline to finish the "Year in Review" is always early December, so I have to make most of December up, but that's not a big concern as I also make up large chunks of the rest of the year.

The book you hold in your hands contains my reviews of all the years of the Second Millennium so far. As a bonus, this book also includes my review of the First Millennium, covering the years 1000 through 1999.[5] These two millenniums have not been picnics for the human race. But as you read this book and review the many tragedies that have befallen humanity over the years, I suspect that you'll come to the same

---

[4] We're talking about dead turkeys here.

[5] I realize that there are people who will argue, convincingly, that, technically, the Second Millennium did not end until the end of the year 2000. To those people I say, in all sincerity: Shut up.

surprising conclusion that I did: No matter what challenges we face as a species—no matter what hurdles are placed in our way—somehow we always find a way, even in the darkest hour, to make things worse. It's a miracle, really. You read about the events of one year and you think, "There is no possible way that human beings can get any stupider than that." Then you read what we did the next year and darned if we didn't pull it off!

Anyway, I hope you enjoy the book. I could not have done it alone. I would like to thank the famous dead British historian Arnold J. Toynbee. I have never read any of his books, but I like the way his name sounds. *Toynbee Toynbee Toynbee.* I would also like to thank Aretha Franklin, for obvious reasons. Last but definitely not least, I thank the members of the Downingtown Area Regional Sewer Authority for all that they have done, and continue to do.

Y1K

DAVE BARRY'S COMPLETE HISTORY OF THE MILLENNIUM, GIVE OR TAKE THREE CENTURIES

And so we stand together—the human race, plus the members of Limp Bizkit—poised on the brink of the year 2000.

In a matter of days, we will find ourselves in a new millennium, facing exciting challenges and questions, such as: Why are we lying in a Dumpster naked? And when did we get this highly personal Pokemon tattoo?

But this is not the time to think about our New Year's Eve plans. This is the time to take one last, lingering look back at the millennium that is drawing to a close. For as the ancient Greek historian Thucydides often said, when he was alive,

"History is a bunch of things that happened in the past." His point was that human civilization is a journey, and only by retracing the steps of that journey can we truly come to know, as a species, where we lost our keys.

And so let us now press the REWIND button on the VCR of time. Let us travel back together, back a thousand years, back to . . .

JANUARY 1, 1000

. . . This was the historic day that humanity celebrated the dawn of our current millennium. The occasion was marked by feasting, dancing, and the public beheading of a whiny, tedious group of people who would not stop insisting that, technically, the new millennium did not begin until January 1, 1001.

But it was not all fun and games back in those days. It was a world of ignorance and fear; a world of pestilence and famine; a world of extremely high b.o. levels. Also there was "the Y1K problem"—an unforeseen manufacturing glitch that caused parchment to malfunction such that many words were turned inside out (OTTO, for example, became TOOT).

Fortunately, back then almost nobody could read, so most people were able to continue doing their jobs under the popular economic system of the time, feudalism, which is sometimes called "the Internet of the Middle Ages." Feudalism was based on a "ladder type" of organizational structure, similar to

Y1K DISASTER

Amway. You started out on the bottom rung, in the position of serf. This was not an easy job, but if you worked hard, followed the rules, did not complain, and were a "team player," after a certain period of time you fell off the bottom rung and died.

This system freed the people higher up on the ladder to form noble families and create new empires, which began ebbing and flowing all over the place—in the words of the great British historian Thomas Carlyle—"like MoonPies on a hot sidewalk." In Asia, the Chinese had just invented gunpowder, which would have made them the strongest military power in the world, except that they had not yet invented guns. Their tactic was to make a pile of gunpowder on the ground, try to trick their enemies into standing on top of it, and then set it off with sparks, thus blowing the enemy up. This tactic only worked against really stupid enemies, so the Chinese did not become a major power until the year 1083, when they developed both the cherry bomb and the bottle rocket, using plans apparently stolen from the Los Alamos National Laboratory.

In western Europe, the two dominant cultures were the French and the English, who hated each other because of a bitter, centuries-old dispute over the right way to prepare food. The French, led by the French warrior Maurice LeBeurre, repeatedly attempted to invade England and forcibly introduce the use of sauces. The English, led by King Harold the Comically Monikered, resisted valiantly until 1066, the year of the Norman Conquest, so called because England became the sole possession of a man named Norman, who has owned it ever since.

Another big conflict was started in 1095, when Pope Urban II (son of Mr. and Mrs. Pope Urban I) launched the Crusades to get the Holy Land back from the Infidels (so called because they wore jackets that said INFIDELS across the back). Over the next two centuries, courageous knights wearing gleaming armor suits would periodically set off from Europe, traveling by day and spending each night in a Motel

VI, until finally, after years of hard journeying, they reached the Holy Land, where they instantly cooked like eggs in a microwave. The Infidels thought this was hilarious.

"They wear METAL?" they'd say. "In THIS climate?"

Meanwhile, in Scandinavia, Viking adventurers (or, as they called themselves, "Norsepersons") were looking for new lands where they could loot, rape, pillage, and eat without utensils. The most legendary of these was Leif Eriksson, who was the son of the legendary Erik the Red, who was the son of the legendary Eric the Mauve, who was the first one to think of wearing a hat with horns. Leif and a hardy crew set sail from Greenland, and finally after many harrowing weeks at sea, during which they almost perished, discovered a new land. It turned out to be Canada, so they went home. After that things remained fairly quiet until the early . . .

1200s

. . . when a Mongol named Genghis Khan (son of Murray and Esther Khan) organized the rest of the Mongols into a fierce horde and took over China by thundering across it on big, scary horses that did not care where they went to the bathroom. Khan and his descendants created a vast empire that ultimately encompassed all of Asia, Asia Minor, Asia Minor Phase II, and the Shoppes at Asia Minor Plaza.

The Mongol Empire had little contact with Europe until

it was visited in 1271 by the Italian traveler Marco Polo, who stayed in China for seventeen years before returning to Venice with two thousand little packets of soy sauce. This led to increased trade between Europe and the East that ultimately came to involve soup, egg rolls, and any two dishes from Column B.

Meanwhile, in England, the English noblemen had become involved in a big dispute with King John over the issue of whether or not he should be required to reveal his last name. This led to a big showdown in 1215 (known to English schoolchildren as "The Big Showdown of 1215") that resulted in the signing of the historic Magna Carta, which is the foundation of the modern legal system because it guaranteed, for the first time, that the noblemen had the right to habeas corpus (literally, "wear tights").

But the good times did not roll for long. In 1337, France, which was then under King Philip VI, was invaded by England, which was then under King Edward III, who had vowed to kill any monarch with a higher Roman numeral. This led to the Hundred Years' War, which, because of delays caused by equipment problems, is still going on.

Matters were not helped any by the arrival of the bubonic plague, or "Black Death," which in the fourteenth century spread throughout Asia and Europe, in the words of the great historian Arnold Joseph Toynbee, "like the plague or something." In those ignorant times, it was believed that the plague was caused by evil spirits. Now, thanks to modern science, we know that the real cause was tiny germs, which were carried by fleas, which in turn were carried by rats, which in turn were eaten by cats, which are in fact evil spirits. The plague killed about one-third of the total European population. It was not covered by HMOs.

Elsewhere in the world, important strides were being strode. In South America, the Aztecs had invented a highly sophisticated calendar; it consisted entirely of weekends, and that was the last anybody heard of the Aztecs. In North America, the indigenous peoples, who called themselves "Native Americans," were building hundreds of mounds, and you will just have to ask them why. Meanwhile, way out on a tiny speck of land in the Pacific that we now call Easter Island, giant, mysterious stone heads were being erected. This was done by teenagers. They'd erect one and then hide in the bushes and wait for the homeowner to come out and see it and yell, "Dammit, Marge, those kids have erected a giant stone head on the lawn again! We're moving off this island!" This led to the development of Polynesia.

Speaking of developments, the "hot trend" sweeping through Europe in the early . . .

1400s

. . . was burning people at the stake, which had become the punishment for just about every infraction, including jousting without a permit. By the 1430s, so many people had been burned at the stake that Europe ran out of stakes and had to start burning people at the lump of peat, which took forever. Eventually, the fuel was exhausted, and the Dark Ages began. Virtually all learning ceased as the great universities of Europe closed their doors (although in response to alumni demand they were able to maintain a full football schedule). It was also around this time that Constantinople was captured by the Ottomans (or, as they were known on parchment, the "Tootmans"). This led to the fall of the Byzantine Empire, an important empire that we should have mentioned earlier.

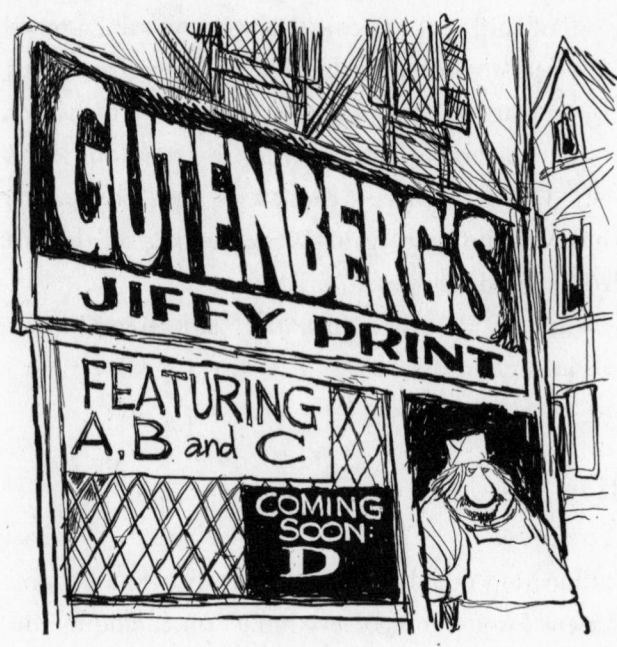

The Dark Ages finally ended when a printer named Johannes Gutenberg had a brilliant idea. In those days, printing was a laborious process because the type was not movable. A typical letter, such as *B,* was four feet high and weighed as much as six thousand pounds. So, to print a book, you had to carry the blank paper around and press it against the letter you needed, one letter at a time; this was slow and tedious, and the printers tended to take shortcuts, as we see by the 1412 edition of the Old Testament, reprinted in its entirety here:

"In the beginning, etc."

One day, Gutenberg had an idea: Instead of moving the paper to the type, why not move the type to the paper? So he tried it, and on a historic day in 1455 three of his assistants were crushed while attempting to lift the letter *W.* So then Gutenberg had the idea of using small type, and within days he printed the first modern mass-produced book, *Codpieces of Passion,* by Danielle Steel.

This led to a rebirth of knowledge that we now call the Renaissance (literally, "Easter Island"). It was spearheaded by the brilliant multitalented Italian Leonardo da Vinci. One day, he was painting a portrait of a young woman named The Mona Lisa when they got to talking in English.

"Leonardo," said The Mona Lisa, smiling enigmatically, "do you think Man will ever be able to fly?"

"I don't know, The," he answered. "But I sure am hungry."

And so he invented pizza, without which the modern world would be a very different place indeed.

But the most important development of the fifteenth century was taking place in Spain and Portugal, which were determined to find a new sea route to Asia. Year after year, they sent ships out into the Atlantic; year after year, they were disappointed. And then they had an idea: Why not put men on the ships to steer them? And thus it was that in 1492 Christopher Columbus sailed from Spain and discovered America, which he believed was the East Indies. The reason he believed this is that prank-loving Vikings, who had discovered America three hundred years earlier, had left a sign that said WELCOME TO THE EAST INDIES!

Nevertheless, as the great historian Edward Gibbon often used to say before passing out, "Once the genie is out of the bottle, the shoe is on the other foot." The Age of Exploration had begun, and by the . . .

1500s

. . . there were ships sailing everywhere, carrying the message of European civilization to the indigenous peoples of Africa and the Americas (the message was: "Hi! We own you!"). Among the greatest mariners of this era was Ferdinand Magellan, who, in 1521, proved that the Earth was round by sailing all the way to the Philippines and getting killed, thus paving the way for what we now know as the tourism industry.

In Asia, many exciting things were happening, but we frankly do not know what they were.

Meanwhile, in Wittenberg, Germany, a priest named Martin Luther nailed ninety-five theses to the church door. This made the church very angry because nobody could read the bingo announcements. As a punishment, Luther was sentenced to the Diet of Worms, which was so disgusting that he started the Protestant Reformation. This movement got a boost in 1534 when Henry VIII started the Church of England after the pope refused to let him divorce his first wife, Elizabeth Taylor.

Henry went on to have a number of wives, most of whom died in freak guillotine accidents. The next major monarch was Mary Tudor, who was known as "Bloody Mary" because she invented the celery garnish. She was succeeded by Elizabeth I, who is the mother of the current queen and is still periodically seen blinking into TV news cameras on her birthday. She presided over the Elizabethan Era, which produced the immortal William Shakespeare, who wrote such timeless works as *Richard II, Richard III, Richard III Strikes Back,* and *Hamlet Hears a Who,* and who gave us a priceless legacy of famous phrases that, to this very day, are pretty much incomprehensible.

The major world power at this time was Spain, which was ruled by King Philip II (or, for short, "King Philip I"), who was legendary all over Europe because of the unnaturally large size of his armada. ("Hey," he was always saying to women, "want to see my armada?") Then, in 1588, the English fleet snuck up and set Phil's armada on fire, and that was pretty much all she wrote with regard to Spain being a major world power.

Meanwhile, exciting progress was being made in Russia, which had decided, after centuries of operating under the Marauding Horde System of government, to switch over to the Lone Homicidal Psychopath System, choosing as its first leader Ivan the Terrible (son of Becky the Terrible). And speaking of progress, in the . . .

1600s

. . . humanity's understanding of the universe took a giant leap forward. It had long been theorized that the Earth orbited around the sun, but there had been no proof until one night in 1609 when an astronomer named Galileo, who had just invented a new device called the "telescope," peered through it and discovered that he could see directly into the bedroom window of a woman who lived nearly five hundred feet away. As a result, many guys became interested in astronomy. Or so they told their wives.

Another important scientific advance occurred in 1614 when the logarithm was invented by Scottish mathematician

John Napier. Someday, when time travel is invented, high-school students will go back and kill him.

But the greatest scientific advance of the century came in 1687, when Sir Isaac Newton, after watching an apple fall off a tree, wrote his famous *Principia Mathematica,* which states that there is a universal force, called "gravity," inside apples. Later scientists would expand this definition to include grapefruit, but the basic concept remains unchanged to this day.

On the political front, 1618 marked the beginning of the Thirty Years' War, in which the German Protestants joined forces with France, Sweden, Denmark, Wisconsin, and the San Diego Chargers to fight against the old Holy Roman Empire, which was led by the Hapsburgs (Stan and Louise). The fighting went on until 1648, when the combatants realized that they would either have to stop fighting or change the name of the war. This led to the Peace of Westphalia, under which the various parties formally agreed that the letters in HOLY ROMAN EMPIRE could be rearranged to spell O RIPEN MY ARMHOLE, thus paving the way for Europe as we know it today.

At this time, France was experiencing its glory years under Louis XIV, who became known as the "Sun King" because he was more than two million miles in circumference. But things were not so good for England, which in 1665 suffered through the Great Plague of London, which was followed in 1666 by the Great Fire of London, which was followed in 1667 by the first recorded attack on London by Godzilla.

Nevertheless, there was hope, and that hope was focused

on the New World, where a group of hardy settlers had founded the first permanent English colony in Jamestown, Va., where the Native Americans introduced them to a local plant with broad leaves. The Virginians found that when these leaves were cured, shredded, and smoked in a pipe, they tasted terrible.

"That's because it's corn, you morons," pointed out the Native Americans. So things looked bad for the colonists, but then they discovered tobacco, which was not as bad, and which was introduced to consumers back in England via a media campaign using the slogan "Tobacco—Eventually, You Stop Throwing Up." This marked the dawn of modern marketing.

Meanwhile, two other famous settlements were being established farther up the North American coast. One was an island on the north end of what we now call New York Bay, which the Dutch settler Peter Minuit purchased from the Manhattan Indians for $24, plus $167,000 a month in maintenance fees. Minuit named this settlement "New Amsterdam," although after it was taken over by the English it became known by the name that has become synonymous with urban greatness: "Easter Island."

The other famous settlement was of course Plymouth Colony, which was founded by Puritans, a group of religious separatists who sailed across the Atlantic in search of a place where they could starve to death. In the winter of 1620, they landed in Massachusetts, where they signed the Mayflower

Compact, in which they swore before Almighty God that if they managed to survive the winter and create a viable colony, and if that colony prospered and grew to the point where, someday, it boasted a major city with a professional baseball team, and if that baseball team was stupid enough to trade away the greatest hitter of all time, then that team would never again win a World Series. And that is why we celebrate Thanksgiving.

In Asian news, the big story was that Peter the Great became the leader of Russia. And if you have to ask why, then you clearly have not stopped to ask yourself how a person gets a nickname like "Peter the Great."

And speaking of great, the . . .

1700s

. . . were a time of important worldwide advances in knowledge that became known, collectively, as "the Enlightenment" because people became so excited that they lost weight. To name just a few advances:

- In England, a chemist named Daniel Rutherford discovered nitrogen, without which many of us would not be here today.
- In France, the great philosopher Voltaire wrote his masterpiece, *Candide,* which tells the fascinating story

of somebody named Candide. At least, that is our assumption.

- In Germany, a composer named Johann Sebastian Bach was writing some hot new fugues, including "Just Fuguen' Around," which was to remain No. 1 on the European Fugue Parade for the next 238 years.

- In Austria, a four-year-old prodigy named Wolfgang Amadeus Mozart sat down at the harpsichord and began to play music in a style so original and exquisite that his father, Walter "Bud" Mozart, smacked him on the head and told him to go outside and play like the other boys, thus paving the way for what would one day become Little League.

- In Scotland, an inventor named James Watt was sitting in his laboratory, looking at an engine and trying to figure out how to make it go, when he decided to brew himself some tea. So he put a teapot on the fire, and when the steam came billowing out Watt had an idea: Wouldn't it be great if you could heat tea water just by plugging something into the wall? So he invented the watt.

- In America, Benjamin Franklin wrote *Poor Richard's Almanack*, which tells the fascinating story of somebody named Candide.

- In Egypt, soldiers discovered the Rosetta Stone (daughter of Sol and Esther Stone). This was very significant because it enabled scholars, for the first time, to decipher ancient Egyptian hieroglyphics, which turned out to be a letter from Publishers Clearing House informing the ancient Egyptians that they might already have won two hundred sheep.

But this was also a century of great turmoil and radical change, and the center of that change was the New World, where, in the words of the great historian Charles Howard McIlwain, "the American colonies, having for too long been forced to consume the bean dip of tyranny, were preparing to release a mighty wind of liberty into the world."

Trouble had been brewing for some time. In 1735, a New York newspaper publisher named John Peter Zenger was arrested after he printed a story alleging that the New York governor had been seen at a Times Square peep show in which milkmaids allegedly operated churns topless (the headline was LUV GUV IN BUTTER FLUTTER). Zenger was acquitted, thus establishing Freedom of Speech and laying the groundwork for what would ultimately become Jerry Springer.

This was followed by the French and Indian War, which further heightened tensions because, contrary to what the name "French and Indian War" suggests, both the French and the Indians were on the same side. Then, in 1765, the British Parliament passed the Stamp Act, which decreed that if the colonists wanted to buy stamps they had to wait in long lines at inconveniently located postal facilities staffed by surly clerks who periodically went on murderous rampages with semi-automatic muskets.

But the straw that finally pushed the camel over the edge of the cliff and caused the dam to burst came in 1773, when the British Parliament placed a tax on tea. In retaliation, a group of Boston patriots dressed up as Indians, sneaked aboard a ship, and threw its cargo into Boston Harbor. Unfortunately, this was a cruise ship and the cargo consisted of retired couples, many of whom were poor swimmers. But the die had been cast, and there was no way to put the shoe back on the other foot. The hostility between the colonies and the British government, headed by King Big Fat Stupid III, was bound to turn into violence, and, finally, on the fateful night of April 18, 1775, the Revolutionary War began when Paul Revere made his legendary "midnight ride," galloping all the way from Boston to Lexington while shouting the message that would resound through the annals of history: "I CAN'T STOP MY HORSE!"

This rallying cry united the colonies, which decided to hold a Continental Congress in Philadelphia, where, on July 4, 1776, the delegates, after passionate debate, signed the Gettysburg Address. To lead the Revolutionary Army, they chose a man named George Washington, who was known and respected throughout the colonies because his picture was on the dollar. Washington scored many important victories, most notably on the dark and bitter cold Christmas night of 1776, when he set out across the Delaware River in a small boat and, after several anxious minutes, discovered land, which he named "New Jersey," after his mother.

Finally, after many historic battles whose names all American schoolchildren should be forced to memorize before they are allowed to buy one more damn Pokemon card if you want our frank opinion, the British surrendered. At last, after years of oppression, all Americans were truly free! (Except for the slaves.)

Soon the delegates to the Constitutional Convention were hard at work, and in 1788 the constitution they created underwent formal ratification, a complex legal procedure involving actual rats. And thus was born a new nation—a nation that would grow and prosper and ultimately become the mightiest nation that the world had ever seen, a shining beacon of hope that today is known throughout the world as "Easter Island."

This new spirit of freedom spread, in the words of the historian William Hickling Prescott, "like crazy." It reached across the Atlantic Ocean to Europe, where the French, warmly embracing the concept of democratic self-government, brotherhood, and equality under the law, whacked many people's heads off.

Yes, the times, as Bob Dylan (1746–present) once observed, were a-changing. And the pace of that change would only increase in the . . .

1800s

. . . which started off with a "bang" in the form of the Louisiana Purchase, in which Thomas Jefferson bought 828,000 square miles from the French for just $15 million, including all appliances. (The French originally wanted $30 million, but they came way down on price when Jefferson pointed out that the parcel included North Dakota.) The newly acquired territory was then explored by two brothers, Lewis and Clark Expedition, who spent two arduous years traveling through the uncharted wilderness, forced to eat virtually every meal at the International House of Jerky. Finally, the Expeditions returned to Washington and presented Jefferson with a map that was amazingly accurate down to the smallest detail, because it was a map of Germany. And that was the beginning of the Interstate Highway System.

But the fledgling nation was soon to find its very existence threatened with the outbreak of the War of 1812 (1807–10), during which the British marched into Washington, D.C., and, with the help of local residents, burned the Internal Revenue Service to the ground. Tragically, it was rebuilt, and eventually the British went back to England, where many of them still reside today. Fed up with this type of foreign interference, the fifth president of the United States, Monroe Doctrine, issued a decree stating that anybody wishing to invade the United States had better have a valid permit.

Meanwhile, over in Europe, Napoleon Bonaparte had himself crowned emperor of France in recognition of the fact that he alone, among all the French, could rearrange the letters in his name to spell RENT AN ABALONE POOP. Through a series of brilliant military campaigns, he went on to conquer a large area of Europe, only to meet his Waterloo in the Battle of Bunker Hill. He was then exiled to Easter Island, where he invented the cream-filled puff pastry that we know today, in his memory, as the Hostess Twinkie.

A few years later, England and China got into the Opium War, during which soldiers on both sides spent most of the time lying around staring at candles and going, "Wow!" England at this point had a new queen, Victoria, who was much beloved despite having basically the same facial expression as a grouper. She reigned for the next 150 years, during which the sun never set on the British Empire, which as you can imagine experienced an alarming increase in skin growths.

Meanwhile, a great Industrial Revolution was taking place, thanks to a cavalcade of technological and scientific advances:

- In 1807, an American inventor named Robert Fulton put a steam engine aboard a ship called the *Clermont*. Needless to say, it sank like an anvil, thus confirming the widespread scientific belief that gravity was still working.
- In 1808, a German musician named Ludwig "van" Beethoven revolutionized the tedious, labor-intensive task of composing when he harnessed a steam engine

to a symphony-making machine, which cranked out Beethoven's fifth, sixth, seventh, eighth, and ninth symphonies in just twelve minutes before exploding, leaving Beethoven permanently deaf, and foreshadowing the music we now call "hip-hop."

- In 1825, a British company came up with the idea of attaching a steam-powered locomotive to a train of passenger coaches. Tragically, this did not float any better than the steamboat did.

- In 1834, a mechanical "analytical engine"—the great-great-grandparent of today's computers—was invented by English mathematician Charles Babbage. He died in 1871, still waiting to talk to somebody from Technical Support.

- In 1844, American inventor Samuel F. B. Morse demonstrated that if he sent an electrical current along a wire, he could cause a magnetic device at the other end to make a series of clicking noises. These noises made no sense to him, so, following the common practice of the time, he attached his device to a steam engine. The rest is history.

But even as these advances were being made, the United States was like a luxury cruise ship drifting toward a hidden iceberg of war, soon to erupt with a bitter brew of hatred that would spill over onto the white linen tablecloth of the nation's consciousness like a slap in the face with a dead flounder. The trouble began in 1836, when legendary frontier figures Davy Crockett, Jim Bowie, and Roy Rogers were killed while defending the Alamo, a horse-rental agency, from an army of irate Mexican businessmen protesting what they perceived as outrageous refueling charges. This led to the Mexican War, which ended in 1848 with the United States getting Texas, California, and all future rights to Salma Hayek.

But the ensuing peace was to be short-lived. The issue of slavery was tearing the United States apart, fanned into flames by the publication of Harriet Beecher Stowe's *Uncle Tom's Cabin,* which told the dramatic story of evil slave overseer Simon Legree's obsessive hunt for a giant albino whale. In 1858, two Illinois candidates for the U.S. Senate, Abraham Lincoln and Stephen Douglas, held seven historic debates moderated by Regis Philbin, who declared Lincoln the winner when he correctly answered the question "When did Johann Strauss compose 'The Blue Danube' waltz?" (Lincoln's answer: "Not yet.")

In 1860, Lincoln ran for president (slogan: "He's Taller Than You") and was elected, only to see the nation rent asunder in 1861 by the Civil War, starring Clark Gable as Rhett Butler. America descended into a long, dark nightmare as brother fought against brother. As you can imagine, this drove their mother crazy.

"You boys stop fighting RIGHT NOW!" she would yell.

But they would not listen, and the nightmare continued until 1865, when the South surrendered, and the slaves, after so many years of bondage and oppression, were finally free to get beat up a lot. The bruised and battered nation was running on a wobbly treadmill, and matters were only made worse when Lincoln, while attending a play, was fatally shot by an actor named John Wilkes Booth. This tragedy led to the passage of a federal law, still in effect today, requiring actors to use blanks.

But despite the disrupting influence of war, progress continued:

- In 1859, English naturalist Charles Darwin published his groundbreaking work *Origin of Species,* in which he theorized that life evolves, through natural selection, from lower and cruder to higher and more sophisticated levels, except in Kansas.
- In 1869, the Suez Canal was finally completed, which meant that for the first time ships could go from wherever the Suez Canal started to wherever it ended, something that had not been possible before.
- In 1876, inventor Alexander Graham Bell spoke into his new invention, the telephone, and transmitted history's first voice message over a wire to his assistant in another room: "Watson, hold my calls." The modern business era had begun.
- In 1877, inventor Thomas Alva Edison leaned over a device and recited "Mary Had a Little Lamb" in a loud and clear voice. Nothing happened, because the device was

a pencil sharpener. Embarrassed, Edison vowed that one day he would invent an electric light so he could see what the hell he was doing.

- In 1896, inventor Guglielmo Marconi patented the wireless telegraph and set up the world's first broadcasting station, which began transmitting a format advertised as "Easy Listening Morse Code."

But then, just when everything seemed to be going great, bang, the U.S. battleship *Maine* blew up and sank in Havana Harbor in what became known as "The Shot Heard 'Round the World," and the Spanish-American War broke out. The U.S., determined to liberate Cuba from Spanish control, dispatched the famous "Rough Riders," who were led by Theodore Roosevelt in the legendary charge up San Juan Hill, only to enjoy a hearty laugh at their own expense when they realized that San Juan was in Puerto Rico. Historians believe this is the first known instance of the Central Intelligence Agency in action.

And speaking of action, things REALLY started heating up for humanity in general once we entered the . . .

1900s

. . . which had historic events occurring left and right, starting in 1901, when Queen Victoria died, although nobody noticed this until 1907. Meanwhile, in the United States, Theodore Roosevelt became president and began building the Panama Canal, which would one day connect Panama with Albany, N.Y.

But an even more important thing happened on December 17, 1903, in Kitty Hawk, N.C.: two bicycle mechanics named Wilbur and Orville Wright Brothers, who as boys had dreamed of building a flying machine so they could drop bombs on the kids who laughed at them for being named "Wilbur" and "Orville," successfully tested the first airplane. It took off with Wilbur at the controls and a flight attendant named Nancy clinging to the undercarriage with one hand while using the other hand to fling packets of honey-roasted peanuts, one of which struck Wilbur in the eyeball, causing him to dive and crash into the first commercially successful automobile, which coincidentally was being tested at Kitty Hawk by Henry Ford. The Transportation Age had dawned.

It was also an Age of Exploration, as bold adventurers ventured to the far corners of the Earth to check it out. In 1909, Robert E. Peary reported that he had reached the North Pole; in 1911, Roald Amundsen reported that he had reached the South Pole; and, in 1913, Walter M. Fleemotz of Decatur, Ga., reported that he had discovered the West Pole in his basement.

Yes, these were exciting times, but it is important to remember that the Russo-Japanese War (1904–5) was, in the words of historian James Mill (1773–1836), "not a weenie roast." The same can be said for the maiden voyage of the British ocean liner *Titanic,* which, while crossing the North Atlantic in 1912, struck an iceberg, which sank to the bottom with all aboard. This tragedy led to strict new laws against carrying passengers on icebergs.

But even that was not enough to prevent Europe from plunging into World War I, which caused so much bitterness that traces of it still linger in certain European waiters. At first, the United States was not involved, but in 1916 Woodrow Wilson was reelected to the presidency with the popular slogan "He Kept Us Out of War," leaving him with no option but to get us into it. Finally (we are skipping some parts here), the war ended, and the League o'Nations was formed to make sure that the world would never, ever, ever again go to war until everybody had acquired bigger weapons.

On a more upbeat note, the Russians, after centuries of oppression, finally got rid of the Czar System of government and switched to the Communist Dictator System, epitomized by Joseph Stalin, who came to power with the popular slogan "He Wants to Kill Pretty Much Everybody."

Important governmental changes were also taking place in the United States, which in 1919 and 1920 passed two historic constitutional amendments:

- The 18th Amendment, which banned alcoholic beverages. This worked liked a charm. All of a sudden, *bang,* everybody stopped drinking alcoholic beverages! And there was no crime! This paved the way for the War on Drugs.

∘ The 19th Amendment, which gave women the right to vote (for men).

In the arena of scientific progress, a German-born physicist named Albert Einstein was thinking up things that were so amazing they made his hair stick out. In 1915, he developed his General Theory of Relativity, which holds that the equivalence of gravitational and inertial mass in the space-time continuum contributes to the quantum perihelion Brownian motion of submolecular particles, which is why eating cheese makes you get stopped up. This knowledge was to prove vital in making the atomic bomb.

The years 1920 through 1929 are often referred to collectively as the "Roaring Twenties" because the name of each year has "twenty" in it. And it is not hard to understand why when we look at some of the events that occurred during this tumultuous decade:

∘ The great American writers F. Scott Fitzgerald and Ernest Hemingway threw up about five thousand times apiece.

∘ Not to mention Babe Ruth.

∘ A lanky young aviator named Charles Lindbergh astounded the world when he took off from New York and landed, fourteen hours later, back in New York, because he had to go to the bathroom. And that is why today we have toilets on planes.

○ Al Jolson starred in the first "talking" motion picture, *The Jazz Singer Strikes Back,* also featuring Charlton Heston as the young Yoda.

Yes, the nation was riding high, but in 1929 it came apart, in the words of the French economist François Quesnay, "like a club sandwich without toothpicks" when the stock market

crashed because of rumors that there would be no such thing as the Internet for more than fifty years. The nation was plunged into the Great Depression, which resulted in joblessness, homelessness, poverty, hunger, and literally millions of Shirley Temple movies, traces of which can still be seen today. In desperation, the nation turned to Franklin Delano "Teddy" Roosevelt, who, in 1933, started the New Deal, a group of massive government programs designed to guarantee Americans that they would never again be without massive government programs.

But there was trouble ahead, and it spelled its name "Adolf Hitler." His evil treachery at Pearl Harbor forced America into World War II, and when it was finally over, there was dancing in Times Square until somebody said, "Hey! Stop dancing! The Cold War has started! Also, somebody took my wallet!" And it was true. The two great superpowers—the United States of America and the Union of United Soviet Socialism Godless Red Communists of Russia—were staring eyeball-to-eyeball through an Iron Curtain in a nuclear confrontation that pitted brother against brother. It was only a matter of time before "Korea" became a household name.

And yet, at the same time, there were bright spots. In 1947, a courageous young athlete named Jackie Robinson became the first African American to break the sound barrier and the Space Age dawned. There was also hope in the Middle East, where the state of Israel was born in a happy celebration highlighted by festive artillery fire that is still going on in some areas.

By the 1950s, America had entered a period of conservatism and conformity under the administration of its grandfatherly war-hero president, Ed Sullivan. But all that was to change when a young Mississippi truck driver named Elvis Presley appeared on national TV, wiggling his hips and wowing the nation's youngsters with a revolutionary new trend that was to become, over the next five decades, the dominant cultural force in the world: the hula hoop. In response, the Russians launched a satellite named *Sputnik* (Russian for "I spit on your knickers"), which flew into space and shot down an American U2 spy plane piloted by a promising young actor named James Dean. Shocked and confused, the American voters turned to younger leadership in the form of John F. Kennedy, and what happened next was, to quote the eloquent historian Thomas B. Macaulay, "bad."

Assassinations. Vietnam. Civil rights. Woodstock. Watergate. Romilar brand cough syrup. These are words that took on new meaning as the era that became known as "the sixties" engulfed the nation in a tidal wave of events that occurred. But finally it was over, and the nation entered an exciting new era, which became known as "the seventies," during which nothing happened. Then came "the eighties," which lasted until 1989, when the people of East Berlin, fed up with decades of oppression and deprivation, tore down the Berlin Wall in response to rumors that it contained DoveBars.

This caused the Soviet Union to collapse, leaving the United States as the world's only superpower. And in the

nineties, this nation has become even more dominant under the leadership and guidance of President Monica Lewinsky. Today, as we stand on the brink of the year 2000, we are a nation of almost unimaginable wealth. Everywhere we look, we see rich people: millionaire athletes, billionaire dot-com Internet geeks, people on TV quiz shows becoming millionaires by answering questions so easy that they would not stump a reasonably alert stump. And although this makes us want these people to get hit by cement trucks, it also makes us realize that we have come a long way in the past thousand years.

And so this New Year's Eve, when the clock strikes twelve, raise a glass to toast the millions of our ancestors who went before us, paving the way for the safe and secure civilization that we enjoy today. Then, when the clock strikes thirteen and the lights go out, start your generator and load your gun.

2000

GEORGE AND AL'S
BIG CHADVENTURE

Looking back on the year 2000, we have to say that, all things considered, it was pretty good.

No, hold it! We just received some late returns in from the 159th manual recounting of the ballots of Palm Beach County, and it turns out that, by a slim margin, it was actually a bad year. So we're glad that it's finally . . .

Whoops! Hold it! We have just been informed that a Florida court has reversed a ruling overturning an earlier court ruling that upheld a previous ruling that rejected an appeal of a ruling that overturned an earlier reversal of an upheld rejection of the decision to count ballots marked only by drool, which means that the year 2000 was . . .

OK, to be honest, we're not sure what kind of year it was. We're not sure of ANYTHING anymore, except that we never, ever, ever want to have another presidential election like this one. We think that everybody who had anything to do with this election, including the entire state of Florida, should be banned from the political process for life. We especially think that all the lawyers involved should be marooned on a desert island, surrounded by man-eating sharks, from which the only escape would to be to build a raft out of severely dimpled chads.

But setting aside the Election from Hell, there were some bright spots in the year 2000:

- NASDAQ went deep into the toilet, which meant we heard a LOT fewer stories about twenty-two-year-old dot-com twerps making $450 million for starting companies that never actually produced anything except press releases.
- The federal budget surplus got so huge that experts believe it could take Congress as long as eighteen months to blow the entire thing on comically unnecessary pork-barrel projects such as the Museum of Ketchup.
- Toward the end of the year, most people finally stopped thinking that it was clever to say "Is that your final answer?" and "Whassup!"
- You also heard almost nothing about Dennis Rodman.

So, on balance, we're feeling pretty uncertain, in an undecided kind of way, as we take a reflective look back at 2000, which began—as so many years seem to, lately—with . . .

JANUARY

. . . which opens with the entire world braced for the impending Y2K disaster, a story that had received more media hype than global warming and Britney Spears combined, with experts warning the public that the electricity could go out, planes could crash, the economy could collapse and renegade ATMs could roam the streets, viciously attacking pedestrians who were unable to remember their PINs.

As it turns out, the only technology that is actually affected by Y2K is the George Foreman Grill, which, at precisely midnight on New Year's Eve, suddenly starts ADDING fat to foods. Other than that, nothing bad happens, and on New Year's Day, all the "experts" admit that they were wrong and refund all the money they received for giving flagrantly incorrect advice. And the Backstreet Boys win the Rose Bowl.

Meanwhile, the dawn of the twenty-first century is celebrated around the world with extravaganzas in all the great cities, most notably Paris, which uses the Eiffel Tower as a framework for the most spectacular light show ever seen; London, which turns the Thames into a mighty river of fire;

and Warsaw, which unveils the "Millennium Kielbasa"—a nineteen-hundred-foot-long sausage stuffed with more than fifty thousand pounds of high explosive that, when detonated, causes chunks of smoked meat to rain down festively all over central Europe.

In other foreign news, Vladimir Putin takes over as president of Russia, replacing Boris Yeltsin, who is forced to resign on New Year's Eve when the Kremlin runs out of vodka. In his inaugural speech, Putin, a former KGB agent, pledges to work for international understanding and maintain peaceful relations with the United States "until we can refuel our missiles."

The United States turns ownership of the Panama Canal over to Panama. Maritime experts quickly became concerned when Panama, seeking to boost revenue by transforming the aging waterway into a Disney-style tourist attraction, installs a "log flume" section. Pieces of disintegrated freighters are soon washing ashore as far away as Costa Rica.

In South America, the War on Drugs, now entering its thirtieth successful year, gets a nice boost when the United States announces that it is giving $1.3 billion more in aid to Colombia, which ducks into the bathroom eight times during the announcement ceremony.

On the domestic political front, Hillary Rodham Clinton makes the extreme personal sacrifice of actually moving into a house located in the state that she has selected to represent in the U.S. Senate. She pledges to "be a good neighbor for the people of whatever the hell this town is." But the big news is in the Iowa caucuses, from which Al Gore and George W. Bush emerge as winners, despite strong objections from Palm Beach County election officials, who announce that they are not aware of any state named "Iowa."

President Bill Clinton orders a do-it-yourself "Build-a-Legacy" kit via the Internet.

The big story in Miami is the intensifying legal battle over whether six-year-old Elián González will return to his father in Cuba or be allowed to stay in the United States and enjoy the precious, constitutionally protected freedom to be displayed on network television every time he burps. In another South Florida development, state agriculture inspectors learn that eight lime trees in South Florida have been infected with citrus canker. As National Guard troops and tanks pour into the area, a state official states, "We are not ruling out napalm strikes."

In financial news, America Online announces the largest merger in history, in which it will acquire Time Warner in exchange for AOL stock valued at $160 billion, or, a little later in the week, $34.

On a sad note, legendary *Mad* cartoonist Don Martin dies, causing a sad hush to fall over the cartooning world, broken only by a gentle sound, coming from somewhere up above: *SPLOINGGG.*

In sports, the St. Louis Rams defeat the Tennessee Titans 23 to 16 in the Super Bowl. The Titans graciously concede, although Palm Beach election officials announce that, according to their scoring, Tennessee actually won by 257 points.

And speaking of seesaw battles, in . . .

FEBRUARY

. . . the presidential primary campaigns heat up as Al Gore, Bill Bradley, George W. Bush, and John McCain sweep through New Hampshire, then hustle down to South Carolina, then blast out to Wisconsin, then race up to Michigan, then, as a result of a faulty compass, charge deep into Canada, where, before discovering their error, they spend a combined $43 million on TV attack ads and hold several debates, in which Bush repeatedly refers to Canadians as "the Canadish people," and Gore claims that he was born and raised in Montreal.

Meanwhile, Steve Forbes, who has spent untold millions of his own money in a hopelessly unrealistic quest for the presidency, finally comes to his senses and drops out of the race, declaring that he will now devote his energies full-time to becoming a power forward for the Los Angeles Lakers.

President Clinton, after working late many nights in the White House Situation Room, finally finishes building his legacy. He goes to sleep a happy man, only to discover, on awakening, that Buddy, the First Dog, has gotten hold of the legacy and chewed it beyond recognition.

On the financial front, in a chilling example of the grow-

ing menace of cyber crime, unidentified hackers attack several major "e-business" websites, temporarily shutting them down, and thus preventing them from losing money anywhere near as fast as usual. Meanwhile, the Dow Jones Industrial Average continues to slide, dipping below the 10,000 mark for the first time since April of 1999. This causes great concern everywhere except Palm Beach County, where election officials have the Dow pegged at 263,000 and "climbing like a rocket."

In other Florida stories:

- State agriculture officials score an important victory in the War on Citrus Canker when they manage to kill two of the eight suspected lime trees with a four-hour barrage of artillery fire. Unfortunately, they also—"You can't make an omelet without breaking eggs," notes one state official—obliterate 237 homes. During the battle, the six other infected lime trees, aided by Greenpeace volunteers, are able to escape, setting off a statewide manhunt.

- After decades of complaints about the inhumanity of its execution procedures, Florida switches from using the electric chair to lethal injection. Unfortunately, the first effort does not go well, as prison officials report that they cannot figure out "how to get the electricity into the syringe."

- The official entourage surrounding six-year-old Elián González reaches the three-hundred-person mark, eclipsing the long-standing record held by the Mike Tyson entourage. In their continuing effort to show what a happy, normal life Elián is leading, his media advisers begin scheduling two playing-happily-in-the-yard photo opportunities per day for the throng of international news media personnel, some of whom have been pressed against the fence for so long that they will have chain-link indentations in their foreheads for the rest of their lives.

Charles Schulz departs gently and quietly, and a sorrowful world realizes that Charlie Brown will never, ever, kick the football. In sports, Tiger Woods wins the Pebble Beach Pro-Am, the Daewoo Classic, the Liquid-Plumr Open, the Extra-Absorbent Depends Tournament of Champions, and the Nebraska State Spelling Bee. And speaking of winning, in . . .

MARCH

. . . George W. Bush and Al Gore clinch their parties' nominations, thanks to a heartfelt outpouring of money from civic-minded special interest groups responding to the candidates' calls for campaign finance reform. John McCain and Bill Bradley both drop out, with each man declaring his sincere support for the opponent he has spent the past several months likening to pond scum. Remaining in the presidential race are Ralph Nader, representing the Flush Your Vote Down the Toilet Party, and Pat Buchanan, representing the asteroid belt.

President Clinton visits the Franklin D. Roosevelt Presidential Library, and, upon exiting, sets off an alarm. Guards discover a piece of FDR's legacy in one of the president's pockets. Nobody can figure out how the heck it got there.

In economic news, consumers voice increasing concern over rising gasoline prices, which have climbed to record levels in almost every part of the nation except Palm Beach County, where election officials report that unleaded premium is selling for 14 cents a gallon.

In science, medical researchers announce that they have

cloned a $100 bill, and will no longer be dependent upon federal grants.

True item: In the War on Smoking, several states take legal steps to protect major tobacco companies from an anticipated huge damage award in a class action lawsuit. The states need the tobacco companies to stay in business, because, thanks to the tobacco settlement, the states now make more money from the sale of cigarettes than the tobacco companies do. If this makes no sense to you, it's because you're a human, as opposed to a lawyer.

In other product liability news, Smith & Wesson announces that henceforth its handguns will be manufactured so that, when the trigger is pulled, a little stick pops out of the barrel with a flag that says *Bang!* The Clinton administration announces that it will oppose this plan on the grounds that the stick "could poke out an eye."

On Wall Street, the Dow plunges, then soars, then evens out for a little while, then—in a move that alarms many observers—briefly switches to degrees Fahrenheit.

In New York City, Mayor Rudolph Giuliani, angered by charges that the city's police are overzealous, defends the department in a press conference that ends abruptly when a *Daily News* reporter raises his hand and is shot 467 times. A review board later rules that the shooting was justified on the grounds that "there was no way to tell that the finger was not loaded."

Another true item: In a stunning journalism coup, ABC News reporter Diane Sawyer stands on her head AND gets squirted with Silly String by international superstar celebrity news object Elián González. Through these and other professional investigative reporting techniques, Sawyer is able to show, in a heavily promoted exclusive interview, that the six-year-old boy is, in fact, a six-year-old boy.

Elsewhere in Florida:

- The War on Citrus Canker escalates as state agriculture authorities fire more than twenty-three thousand rounds in a shopping mall shoot-out against a gang of renegade orange trees, resulting in numerous civilian casualties. Unfortunately, all the trees manage to get away, but authorities confidently report that one of them "lost a lot of sap."
- Scandal-plagued Miami International Airport suffers yet another setback when inspectors discover that the new air traffic control tower, which has been under construction for two years, is actually a tree fort. "And not a particularly well-built tree fort, either," the inspectors add.
- Dan Marino retires, causing hundreds of sports-talk-radio callers to stop complaining that he stinks and start complaining that the Dolphins are going to really stink without him.

In a major upset at the Academy Awards, the Oscars for Best Film, Best Director, Best Screenplay, Best Actor and Actress, AND Best Supporting Actor and Actress all go to Tiger Woods.

And speaking of drama, in . . .

APRIL

. . . the tension in the Elián González case nears the breaking point as the boy's father flies to the United States and—this is a great country—immediately acquires a nice suit and roughly fifty lawyers. Meanwhile, the U.S. Justice Department demands custody of Elián, only to be shrewdly outmaneuvered by the Miami relatives, whose own lawyer squadron files legal briefs arguing that (1) there is no "Elián González" and (2) he is taking a nap. As tempers flare and street protests turn increasingly ugly, Miami-Dade County mayor Alex Penelas seeks to defuse the situation by sternly declaring that, in the event that people decide to riot, "we certainly won't stand in the way."

The drama reaches its zenith in the predawn hours of April 22 when a team of U.S. Border Patrol officers is able to gain entrance to the Miami relatives' home through the clever ploy of knocking on the door and shouting, "Candygram for the Miami relatives!" The agents burst inside and snatch Elián from the arms of Donato Dalrymple, who has come to be

known as "the Fisherman," because it sounds better than "the Publicity-Grubbing Parasite."

Within hours, the streets of Miami are filled with throngs of people shouting and blocking intersections. This is pretty much normal.

In another landmark legal action, the federal government's marathon antitrust case against Microsoft comes to an end when a federal judge finds the software giant guilty of being successful. In what will prove to be a fateful ruling, the judge orders Microsoft to split into two smaller companies, one of which will continue to make the Windows operating system, and the other of which will immediately begin manufacturing Firestone tires. In response, the NASDAQ, for the first time in its history, closes at exactly equal to *pi*.

On the legacy front, President Clinton, with his official entourage of thirty-five hundred, flies to Tonga in hopes of brokering a historic peace agreement only to discover that, tragically, Tonga is an isolated island nation that has not been at war with anybody for centuries. Tongan officials express regret, and promise to give Mr. Clinton a holler if they spot any hostile-looking canoes or anything.

On a happier note, the 2000 Census goes smoothly, with preliminary results showing a shift in U.S. population from the Rust Belt to the Sun Belt, particularly Palm Beach County, which reports a gain of 157 trillion residents.

In sports, Vijay Singh wins the Masters Golf Tournament and is awarded the coveted green jacket, which is quickly snatched away by angry Buick executives and given to Tiger Woods.

And speaking of competition, in . . .

MAY

. . . the presidential race heats up as George W. Bush proposes an idea, which he came up with recently while reading an index card, that allows younger workers to take some of their Social Security money and, as the governor puts it, "investisize in the stocks market or professional baseball teams or whatever and thusly enjoy the labors of their fruits." Vice President Al Gore immediately criticizes this plan as a "risky scheme" that could result in "millions of dead senior citizens," which, in turn, "could impact global warming." Polls show that this is a hot-button issue with the public, with 50 percent of likely voters wishing they had two other candidates to choose from and the other 50 percent agreeing.

In legacy action, President Clinton flies to Wales, where he holds high-level talks with a number of officials only to be informed that they are members of his own entourage.

In medicine, the American Academy of Pediatrics reports that it has finally tracked down seven-year-old Matthew Parmogaster, believed to be the only remaining boy in the United States not being treated for attention-deficit/hyperactivity disorder (ADHD). A team of camouflage-wearing doctors is able to creep close enough to the youngster to bring him down with Ritalin-tipped blowgun darts.

In business news, United Airlines announces that it intends to purchase US Airways, a move that will enable United, in the words of its official statement, "to nearly double the number of daily flights that we cancel without warning."

Computer networks around the world are temporarily paralyzed by an Internet virus called the "Love Bug," which gets its name from the fact that it causes computers to mate with other types of office equipment. It is eventually brought under control, but not before spawning a host of Mr. Coffee machines capable of playing world-class chess.

In sports, Fusaichi Pegasus wins the Kentucky Derby, whipped to a strong finish by a nine-iron-wielding Tiger Woods.

In conservation news, the National Park Service, concerned about the buildup of unwanted brush in the Los Alamos, N.M., area, decides to solve the problem by setting a fire that burns down 260 homes. "We suspected that these homes might contain unwanted brush," explains a Park Service spokesperson. This bold action does not go unnoticed by Florida citrus canker fighters.

Speaking of bold action, in . . .

JUNE

. . . Vice President Gore unveils his own plan to save Social Security via a complex system of tax credits, grants, loans, stern lectures, and mandatory home composting, which Gore would personally direct via a daily two-hour broadcast from the White House. Texas governor Bush, after being briefed on the Gore plan by aides using hand puppets, dismisses it as "an unwarrantied inclusion upon the whaddycallit." Polls show many voters looking into Norwegian citizenship.

Fears are raised that U.S. security has been seriously breached when the Los Alamos National Laboratory discovers that it has lost its nuclear secrets. Laboratory officials express shock, noting that the secrets were kept in a special

secure box tied shut with two pieces of string and clearly marked NUCLEAR SECRETS! DO NOT TAKE! Fortunately, the mystery is solved a few days later when the secrets are discovered safe and sound in the home of a laboratory worker whose eight-year-old daughter, Amber, had taken them to her elementary school for a special show-and-tell session attended by the second through fourth grades and six special guests from China.

In weather news, the East Coast braces for what experts predict could be a busy hurricane season. Palm Beach County reports four feet of snow.

On a cultural note, the hugely popular TV show *Who Wants to Be a Millionaire* has its first million-dollar winner when an Ohio man correctly answers Regis Philbin's final question: "What color is my tie?" (Answer: "The same color as your shirt.")

On the legal front, the U.S. Environmental Protection Agency announces a ban on molecules, which, according to an agency spokesperson "can join together and form chemicals." Meanwhile, an obviously testy U.S. Supreme Court, in an 8 to 1 ruling, orders Antonin Scalia to stop cracking his damn knuckles.

In a historic international development ending fifty years of Cold War hostility, South Korean president Kim Dae-jung meets with North Korean leader Kim Jong Il. They sign a formal pact in which they agree to henceforth address each other as "Buddy," then flee, escaping a warm Bill Clinton embrace by mere seconds. On a sadder note, Syrian president Hafez Assad dies; in an official statement, Vice President Gore recalls that he and Assad "often raced camels together," while Gov. Bush extends "deepest sympathy for the widow, Mrs. President Syrian."

Jeff MacNelly, a regular guy who was also a genius, leaves this world for one where beer is plentiful, cigars are welcome, and all the cars are 1959 DeSotos.

In sports, the U.S. Open is not actually held because it's more efficient to just mail the check to Tiger Woods.

And speaking of victories . . .

JULY

. . . begins with a stunning upset of the ruling party in the Mexican presidential election, which is won by underdog challenger Vicente Fox, aided by an unexpected 4.3 million votes from Palm Beach County.

In U.S. politics, George W. Bush meets with his top advisers, who inform him that, after careful consideration, he has selected as his running mate Dick "Dick" Cheney, thus balancing the ticket by including a person who speaks at least some English. Bush and Cheney are formally nominated at a convention in Philadelphia featuring a prominent display of minorities, some of whom—in a stark departure from GOP tradition—are not holding hors d'oeuvres trays. The convention is also marked by street demonstrations held by angry young people who hate capitalism and consumerism and are determined to fight these evils until it's time to go back to college.

In legacy action, President Clinton, desperate to forge a lasting Middle East peace, brings Yasser Arafat and Ehud Barak to Camp David. Finally, after two weeks of exhausting round-the-clock negotiations, the talks are broken off because neither man can remember what country he represents.

The U.S. missile defense system suffers yet another setback during a much-publicized test when an interceptor missile, which is supposed to hit a mock warhead high over the Pacific Ocean, instead slams into the newly refurbished Washington

Monument. Military officials, seeking to put a positive spin on the mishap, note that the monument had "a very suspicious shape."

In domestic news, the South Carolina state legislature, in a move that angers the state's traditionalists, votes to abolish slavery.

In Florida courtroom action, the jury in the civil lawsuit against cigarette manufacturers hands down a harsher than expected verdict, ordering a dozen top tobacco executives to be beheaded. In another controversial ruling, a federal judge orders Napster.com, the popular Internet music-exchange site, to "put some Wayne Newton on there."

In cultural news, bookstores around the country are swamped with orders for the fourth Harry Potter book, *Buy This Book or Your Children Will Hate You*. U.S. profits total tens of millions of dollars, all of which will be paid to settle broomstick-related lawsuits.

Walter Matthau goes to that big, messy apartment in the sky. In sports, officials of the Baseball Hall of Fame correct a long-standing oversight by voting to induct Tiger Woods.

And speaking of winners, in . . .

AUGUST

. . . Vice President Gore, in a historic move, selects as his running mate Sen. Joseph Lieberman, who is a member of the

Jewish faith, which Gore cofounded. Lieberman boldly declares that he is in favor of God, and demonstrates this by demanding that the Hollywood community "stop making disgusting and immoral movies" but "please continue to give us money."

Lieberman is seen as a solid choice, but there is tension at the Democratic Convention in Los Angeles, where the Gore camp suspects that Bill Clinton is trying to hog the limelight. A Clinton staffer denies this, claiming that "security considerations" led to the decision to have the president enter the convention hall riding a chariot drawn by lions.

In other entertainment news, *Monday Night Football* debuts Dennis Miller, hired as a color commentator to boost ratings. The first broadcast goes well, as Miller interacts well with play-by-play announcer Britney Spears.

In consumer news, owners of certain models of Firestone tires receive a troubling notice from the manufacturer urging them to "lock yourself in your bathroom immediately." Congress holds emergency hearings, but is unable to get testimony from Firestone tire designers, who are busy working on an improved new ballot for Palm Beach County.

On a positive automotive note, the nation is captivated by the story of eighty-three-year-old Tillie Tooter, who survives three days trapped in her car in a swamp. Police later determine that she was run off the road by Florida state agriculture officials, who suspected she might be carrying infected citrus trees in her trunk. In angry response, a Florida jury orders the tobacco industry to pay another $300 billion in damages.

Speaking of survivors: The summer's surprise hit TV show, *Survivor,* climaxes when the other contestants vote to elect, as the grand prize winner, Richard Hatch, best known for walking around naked. Hours later, in what aides for each side claim is a coincidence, Al Gore and George W. Bush both hold "town hall" meetings in the nude.

Tiger Woods is kidnapped by rival golfers, sedated, handcuffed, placed in a straitjacket, wrapped in chains, and locked inside a trunk, which is then weighted with concrete blocks and dropped into the deepest part of the Pacific Ocean. He easily wins the PGA Championship.

And speaking of crime, in . . .

SEPTEMBER

. . . the Midwest is terrorized by a vicious outlaw gang that robs a string of banks by threatening to put Firestone tires on the tellers' cars.

But the real excitement occurs in the political arena, where Al Gore and George W. Bush spend much of the month sparring vigorously over the critical question—foremost on the minds of every American—of what will be the format for their debates. Gore proposes a series of seventeen debates, fifteen of which would consist entirely of the vice president reading selected portions of his book *Earth in the Balance,* soon to be released as a major motion picture featuring Alec

Baldwin as an endangered species. The Bush camp counters with a proposal for one debate, to consist of a round of horseshoes, man to man, with no talking. The two sides finally settle on three debates: one in the standing format, one in the sitting format, and one with both candidates in a hot tub with Jim Lehrer.

Meanwhile, both Bush and Gore seek to impress the voters with their qualifications to hold the world's most powerful office by appearing on *The Tonight Show with Jay Leno, The Late Show with David Letterman, Late Night with Conan O'Brien, The Oprah Winfrey Show, Judge Judy, Sesame Street, Gilligan's Island, Scooby-Doo,* and—most notably—*Teletubbies,* where Vice President Gore claims that he was the inspiration for Noo-Noo the magic vacuum cleaner, and Gov. Bush, in a controversial move, kisses Tinky Winky on the lips.

On the issues front, Gore proposes that the federal government reduce gas prices by releasing oil from the nation's strategic petroleum reserve, kept in giant salt domes in Louisiana. Despite opposition from Gov. Bush, who criticizes the plan as "an act of fragrant perspiration," President Clinton orders the release of thirty million barrels of oil. The joy of consumer groups soon turns to alarm as a fifteen-foot-high wave of petroleum wipes out Baton Rouge. Everyone agrees this is no big loss.

In another consumer development, Kraft Foods voluntarily recalls millions of taco shells after discovering that some of them contained genetically altered corn. A Kraft spokesperson stresses that the tacos are "perfectly safe," provided that they "are handled properly" and "never allowed near children."

In legal news, the U.S. Justice Department, which has been holding Los Alamos physicist Wen Ho Lee in jail for eighteen months after identifying him as a major atomic spy, announces that it has reduced the charges to two counts of improper parking. Also getting good legal news are Bill and Hillary Clinton, who heave a sigh of relief when the special prosecutor investigating Whitewater announces that, after years of investigation, he has no earthly idea what "Whitewater" is. The president declares that he is "proud and humbled to join the ranks of such big-legacy presidents as George Washington, Abraham Lincoln, and John F. Kennedy, who also were never indicted in connection with Whitewater."

In Florida, state agriculture officials escalate the scope of the War on Citrus Canker to include "any object that is yellow or orange." Within a week, state crews have destroyed five thousand school buses, twenty-seven thousand traffic cones, and Donald Trump's hair. Outraged, a Florida jury slaps another $500 billion in damages on the tobacco companies.

The international highlight of September is the Summer Olympics, which were actually held in Australia in July but are just now reaching the United States. The delay results from the broadcast format chosen by NBC, which has decided to make the Olympics interesting to U.S. viewers by adding soundtracks, breaking away from the competition to show dramatic profiles, and using computers to digitally replace foreign athletes with popular NBC sitcom characters. The highlight of the games, without question, is the thrilling moment when—with the entire Australian nation cheering as if with one voice—the women's 400-meter race is won by *Frasier* star Kelsey Grammer.

Unfortunately, the Olympics also produces some unhappy moments. Suspicions of drug use are raised by the noticeable buildup of syringes on the bottom of the swimming pool. And the women's gymnastics competition is marred when the vault is set to an incorrect height of fifty-seven feet by volunteer officials from Palm Beach County. But all in all it is a fine Olympics, with thirty-nine gold medals going to the United States, thirty-two to the Russian Federation, twenty-eight to China, and 2,038 to Tiger Woods.

Unfortunately, the spirit of international friendship is nowhere to be found in . . .

OCTOBER

. . . when the Middle East again erupts in violence, touched off when a sacred Jerusalem religious site is severely damaged by an errant interceptor missile being tested for the U.S. missile defense system. The Pentagon blames the malfunction on the fact that the missile "was, in violation of proper procedure, equipped with Firestone tires."

In another major international development, massive street

protests in Yugoslavia force the resignation of President Slobodan Milošević, who is replaced by Vojislav Koštunica, who promises to "work toward a day when every Yugoslavian citizen has a pronounceable name." Milošević, ending thirteen years as a dictatorial thug, flees to the United States, where he takes a job in customer service.

Meanwhile, the U.S. presidential campaign reaches a fever pitch as Al Gore and George W. Bush, both of them briefed to the point of incoherence, face off in their three debates. When it's all over, observers agree that each man managed to clearly define himself as the owner of several dark suits. With the polls showing the race to be neck and neck, it becomes clear that the outcome will be determined by undecided voters who, to judge from their post-debate focus groups on network TV, have rock salt for brains. ("Dan, I'm concerned about health care, because I keep wandering into traffic.")

In consumer news, Kraft Foods reports that a genetically altered corn plant has escaped from its laboratories. A Kraft spokesperson warns that the plant should be considered "eared and dangerous."

In Florida, torrential rains bring widespread disaster, as thousands of homeowners are trapped by rising water, forcing state agricultural officials to drop bombs on their citrus trees from helicopters.

In sports, New York City goes nuts over the first "subway" World Series in forty-three years, which is won in convincing fashion by the New York Mets, who, behind the strong relief putting of Tiger Woods, destroy the overpaid Yankees and their obnoxiously arrogant fans. (If you disagree, write your own "Year in Review.")

And speaking of historic clashes, in . . .

NOVEMBER

. . . the U.S. presidential campaign finally stumbles to what everyone believes is the finish line as millions of Americans go to the polls and, in the sacrosanct privacy of the voting booth, exercise the most cherished right of this glorious democracy: the right to screw up their ballots. Hints of trouble surface early in Palm Beach County, where many voters, asked to sign the voter rolls, write their names on floors, walls, each other, etc.

But the real confusion starts on election night, as the major news networks, relying on statistics provided by the Firestone Quality Control Division, first announce that Gore has won Florida; then that Gore has NOT won Florida; then that Bush has won Florida; then that Bush has NOT won Florida; then, briefly, that Florida has settled on the late William Howard Taft. As dawn breaks, confusion reigns; veteran CBS anchor lunatic Dan Rather sums up the situation for his viewers with the old country saying: "This race is like a goose trying to catch a mackerel with a pork chop in his vest pocket and a frying pan on his UHHHHH."

At this point, Rather is, mercifully, felled by a tranquilizer dart, but the rest of the nation is left in a state of confusion regarding the election outcome. Fortunately, this is America and not some unstable Third World nation, so within a matter of hours the confusion is transformed into much, much deeper confusion. The skies darken over Florida as hundreds of thousands of lawyers parachute into the state from bombers supplied by the Bush and Gore campaigns; most have filed lawsuits before they hit the ground.

Soon it is impossible to turn on any TV channel, including the Home Shopping Network, without seeing an expert (defined as "a person wearing makeup") explaining the incredible cosmic complexities of "chads," which are tiny squares of cardboard that contain, hidden somewhere deep in their molecular structure, the intents of voters.

The state is engulfed in court battles, such as the case in Chalupa County, where an election worker fed his Pop-Tart into the ballot-counting machine. The machine registered this as a vote for Pat Buchanan, but Democratic lawyers make a strong case that it clearly intended to vote for Al Gore. Gore himself begins holding hourly round-the-clock press conferences to declare that "in America, every vote must be counted, whether it is a vote for me, or a vote that, if you hold it up to the light and stare at it long enough with very little sleep, appears that it might be for me."

Meanwhile, lawyers for the Bush campaign pull every legal string to prevent any change in the final Florida count, which shows Bush ahead by two votes, both cast by Mr. Waldo Hamperthumper, who lives abroad and whose absentee ballot is postmarked July 3, 1947. Helping the Bush cause is Florida secretary of state Katherine Harris, a Republican, who—in a move that Democrats charge is beyond her legal powers—certifies that Bush has won not only in Florida, but also Ohio, California, and Michigan. While all this is going on, Dick Cheney suffers his forty-third heart attack, but quickly declares through his oxygen tube that he is "feeling fine" and is "ready to resume consulting with Gov. Bush about what he thinks."

The wild uncertainty of the presidential election overshadows some big political news at the state level, most notably the U.S. Senate races in Missouri, which elects a dead person (Orson Welles), and New York, which elects Hillary Clinton, who, in her first official act, hires Brad Pitt as an intern.

In nonelection news:

- Israeli and Palestinian leaders agree to end the violence, then cement the pact by punching each other in the mouth.
- President Clinton visits Vietnam to see if he can create a legacy of healing, but the Vietnamese are too busy setting up McDonald's franchises.
- Kraft Foods reports that the genetically altered corn plant has turned up in Nebraska, where it has taken over an entire farm, barricading itself inside a silo protected by a cadre of vicious and extremely loyal soybeans. The corn plant has issued a series of demands, among them that it be addressed as "Colonel."
- France is overrun by mad cow disease when the French army, sent to stop an incoming shipment of hamburger, instead surrenders to it.

But the really big story remains the presidential election, with tension building to a massive, headache-inducing climax in . . .

DECEMBER

. . . a month packed with so much historic courtroom drama that exhausted TV legal experts start dropping like flies, only to have new experts shove their bodies aside and resume analyzing in midsentence (". . . and so, Bill, depending on how the judge rules here, we could have a situation where the person next in line for the presidency is Alexander Haig"). Every few minutes, around the clock, some court issues a historic ruling overturning a historic ruling issued only moments earlier by some other court. It quickly becomes impossible for anybody to keep track of the situation, as evidenced by an alarming incident involving a sleep-deprived judge in Gazomba County who, after hearing a ballot-tampering case, issues a sloppily worded ruling in which he accidentally sentences himself to death. He is pardoned by Florida governor Jeb Bush, a move that is immediately challenged by Democratic lawyers, who argue that Bush clearly intended to pardon Al Gore.

In another memorable legal event, a truck travels from Miami to Tallahassee carrying a cargo of eight hundred thousand tightly packed Miami-Dade County voters, every single one of whom testifies before Judge Sanders Sauls, who subsequently rules that his name can be rearranged to spell UNDRESS A LASS.

As the month wears on, the Gore legal team suffers a series of setbacks, both in terms of court verdicts and hair days, but the vice president remains upbeat and confident, according to sources within his inner circle of strategists, which has shrunk to Gore and an imaginary kangaroo named "Mr. Woodles." Gore insists that he "will not prolong the election unnecessarily"; he makes this statement at the formal dedication of the new fifty-story Tallahassee headquarters of the Al Gore Florida 2000 Election Lawsuit Institute.

Meanwhile, George W. Bush remains on his ranch, looking as presidential as he knows how. The ranch does not appear to have any plant or animal life; it's just a ranch where top Republicans sit around wearing ranch-style outfits and advising Bush on how to, as the governor puts it, "have a smooth transmission." His first big job is to select his cabinet, which, according to a spokesperson, will be "very diverse, including Americans from every segment of the oil industry." Bush is also briefed by foreign-policy experts, who show the governor a globe, then spend several hours explaining to him why the countries on the bottom don't fall off.

In vice-presidential candidate action, Joe Lieberman, wearing a fake beard, tiptoes back to his senate office. Dick Cheney is diagnosed with citrus canker.

As the deadline looms for picking state electors for the Electoral College, the Florida legislature meets in a controversial emergency session, where the Republican majority, in a move that Democrats charge is unconstitutional, votes to impeach Bill Clinton.

Finally, with all other legal options exhausted, the presidential election mess lands in the lap of the U.S. Supreme Court. After several minutes of deliberation, the court issues a unanimous ruling—hailed by legal scholars as well as the public—that Florida must be given back to Spain.

Spain immediately files an appeal.

And so the year staggers to its conclusion with the nation mired in a toxic swamp of public cynicism and corrosive partisan bitterness that could eat away the foundation of our democracy. And yet, even as earthbound humans wallow in petty squabbles over chads, something wonderful and hopeful is happening in the heavens: the crew of the space shuttle *Endeavour*, piloted by Tiger Woods, completes a major phase in the construction of the international space station—a place where, one day, scientists from around the world will work in harmony for the betterment of mankind.

Hours later, the station is shot down during a test of the U.S. missile defense system.

Happy New Year.

2001

I didn't write a "Year in Review" for 2001. I would have had to write it only a few weeks after 9/11, and at the time it didn't feel right to make jokes about the rest of the year and then either ignore the attacks or suddenly become serious. So I took that year off, although I have no doubt that many stupid things happened.

Speaking of stupid, let's move on to 2002 . . .

2002

AMERICA JUST WANTS TO FOCUS ON ITS SALAD

If you had to pick one word to describe our national mood in 2002, that word would be "wary." We went to sleep wary and we woke up wary. We wallowed in wariness. We were wabbits.

This was partly because bad things kept happening. But it was also because government officials kept issuing alarming, yet vague, warnings. "We have received reliable information," an official would say, "that something bad might happen. We don't know what, or when, or where. But it is very, very bad. Also we are seeing the letter E. So we urge all citizens to continue leading normal lives, while remaining in a state of stark, butt-puckering terror. Tune in tomorrow and we'll see if we can't ratchet this thing up a notch or two."

We were also wary of the stock market. One day it was up, the next day it was down, the next day after that it was way down. And as we watched our 401(k) plans decline from a retirement villa in France to a refrigerator carton in an alley, we heard the unceasing babble of the financial "experts," the ones who have never yet failed to be wrong, speculating endlessly on whether the market had bottomed out:

FIRST EXPERT: Bill, I think we may be seeing the bottom here, unless the market goes lower.

SECOND EXPERT: I agree, Bob. If the market does not go any lower, then this is the bottom. But by the same token, if the market DOES go lower, then this is not the bottom. We can say whatever we want and people will take us seriously, because we're on TV and we're wearing suits.

FIRST EXPERT: I like to say "bottom," Bill. Bottom bottom bottom.

SECOND EXPERT: Ha-ha! But seriously, Bob, if the market goes higher from here, then we can say this is . . .

And so on, day after wary day. We became even warier when we found out that some large corporations had essentially the same business ethics as Bonnie and Clyde. It got so bad that we even became wary of Martha Stewart, who hit her own personal bottom (we are speaking figuratively) during a June appearance on the CBS early-morning show. Martha was trying to chop some cabbage for a salad, and the show's host, Jane Clayson, kept pestering her about her alleged insider trading, and finally Martha emitted what was probably the most poignant quote from all of 2002: "I want to focus on my salad."

In a way, Martha was speaking for the entire nation. We all wanted very much to focus on our salad in 2002. But it was impossible with so many things making us wary. In addition to being wary of terrorism and economic uncertainty, we were wary that our children would be abducted, that a sniper would shoot us, that Saddam Hussein would attack us, or that we would attack him. We were wary of asteroids, wary of wildfires, wary of floods, wary that *American Idol* was fixed, wary of fast food, wary of global warming, wary of Florida elections, wary of professional baseball, wary of the West Nile virus, wary that at any moment, some evil, vicious, sick, twisted mind with no regard for the norms of human decency would decide to make a sequel to *Scooby-Doo*.

But, somehow, one wary day at a time, we got through 2002. Now we are poised to enter a new year, which, according to Wall Street analysts, will be 2003, so we would not bet on it. But before we move ahead to wherever we're going, let us take one last, wary look back at the year just completed, starting with . . .

JANUARY

. . . which begins on a hopeful note in Europe, as the nations of the European Union replace their individual currencies with the new "euro," which is expected to boost the European economy by tricking clueless American tourists—who were just starting to figure out the old currencies—into leaving unintentionally gigantic tips. The euro is an immediate success in Paris, where an elderly Ohio couple orders two coffees at a Paris café and discovers, by the time they have settled the bill, that the waiter now owns their house.

But the economic news is not so good in the United States, where President George W. Bush and the Congress discover that the federal budget surplus, which only moments earlier had been trillions of dollars, is now . . . missing! Everybody looks high and low for it, but the darned thing is just GONE. Iraq is suspected.

In other executive action, the nation gets a scare when President Bush chokes on a pretzel, which is immediately wrestled to the floor by Secret Service agents. The president is unconscious for about thirty seconds, during which time Vice President Cheney appoints 173 federal judges.

But the big domestic issue is Homeland Insecurity, which is most noticeable at airports, where the Department of Transportation, having determined that every single 9/11 hijacker was a young male from a Middle Eastern country, has

implemented a shrewd policy of hassling randomly selected elderly women.

Meanwhile, al-Qaeda fighters captured in Afghanistan are flown to the U.S. Naval Station at Guantánamo Bay, Cuba, for detainment. This outrages various perpetually outraged human rights organizations, which issue a statement charging that the prisoners are being kept under inhumane conditions, including "a lack of even the most rudimentary volleyball equipment."

In other terrorist news, American Taliban fighter John Walker Lindh is hired as a marketing consultant by Major League Baseball.

On a positive military note, specially trained U.S. forces

score a major victory when, after days of brutal fighting, they capture what is believed to be the headquarters of Enron, although they acknowledge that there are probably "many smaller Enron cells still operating throughout the nation." The stock market drops 87 points.

Dave Thomas flips his last burger. In sports, Mike Tyson, appearing before the Nevada Athletic Commission to plead for a boxing license, expresses deep remorse for his past misbehavior, and informs the commissioners that if they turn him down he will have no option but to eat their children. The Department of Homeland Insecurity responds by placing the nation on a Code Fuchsia Alert ("Relatively High").

Speaking of effective tactics, the month of . . .

FEBRUARY

. . . opens with a World Economic Forum meeting in New York City, where angry protesters, determined to rid the world of poverty, hunger, disease, and pollution, attack the obvious root cause of all these problems: The Gap. In other economic news, Argentina, seeking to avert bankruptcy, makes a payment of $27.42 toward its Visa bill, currently $48 billion.

In happier economic news, Americans enjoy the wacky and hilarious spectacle of Enron executives being sternly lectured about financial responsibility by members of the United

States Congress. Meanwhile, President Bush, seeking to reassure Americans concerned about losing their retirement savings in the plunging stock market, proposes a bold series of federal initiatives designed to "develop nutritious, low-cost recipes using peanut butter." The stock market drops 153 points.

In the War on Terrorism, security personnel at Chicago's O'Hare Airport wrestle would-be passenger Merline A. Grelpner, ninety-one, to the ground after an alert screener notices that she is carrying an object that is later confirmed, by the FBI, using spectrographic analysis, to be a pretzel. The Department of Homeland Insecurity places the nation on a Code Magenta Alert ("A Tad Higher Than Relatively High, But Not Totally High").

In sports, the New England Patriots win the Super Bowl, thus using up all the sports luck that New England has been accumulating for decades and thereby guaranteeing that the Red Sox will not win the World Series for another 150 years.

But the big sporting event is the Winter Olympics, which brings thousands of athletes and spectators from around the world to Salt Lake City to celebrate the official Olympic theme: "A Salute to Metal Detectors." The games go smoothly at first, except in the alpine events, where the competitors, their skis having been confiscated by airport security, must slide down the mountain on their butts. But the big scandal occurs in pairs figure skating, where the Canadian team clearly outskates the competition, only to see the gold medal awarded, in a judging decision that creates an international uproar, to . . . Iraq.

And speaking of international tension, in . . .

MARCH

. . . the situation worsens in the Middle East as Israeli tanks, following a series of Palestinian attacks, surround Yasser Arafat's headquarters, cutting off the electricity, telephone service, water, and pizza delivery. This is roughly the twenty-fifth time the Israelis have had Arafat surrounded, but the crafty leader persuades them to let him go by promising to take a shower, a pledge he immediately violates.

Meanwhile, the United States is treated to an amazing but absolutely true Homeland Insecurity development when, on March 11, a Florida flight school receives formal notification from the U.S. Immigration and Naturalization Service that the INS has approved student visas for Mohamed Atta and Marwan al-Shehhi, both of whom are currently deceased, having hijacked airplanes and flown them into the World Trade Center exactly six months earlier. Stung by the intense criticism that follows, the INS director vows that the agency will implement tough new procedures for reviewing visa applications, "including, if necessary, actually reading the names."

In other government action, Congress passes a campaign finance reform law, thus guaranteeing that, henceforth, politicians will not be influenced by money. Also, the sun will rise in the west. Meanwhile, the Whitewater investigation, which lasted six years and cost $70 million, finally comes to a close with the special prosecutor issuing a five-volume report concluding that Hillary Clinton "probably" dyes her hair.

In business news, investigators probing the Enron scandal finally track down the accounting firm of Arthur Andersen, which had sought to evade prosecution by changing its name to "Arthur Smith" and disguising its corporate headquarters with a gigantic red wig and sunglasses. Troops are sent to capture the firm, only to discover that the top auditors have escaped to . . . Iraq. The Department of Homeland Insecurity responds by ratcheting the nation up to a Code Ocher Alert ("Deeply Concerned"). The stock market drops 381 points.

On the religious front, the Catholic Archdiocese of Boston pays $23 million to a man who alleged that his parish priest, on more than a dozen occasions in the 1970s, exposed him to the soundtrack from *Grease,* and now he can't get it out of his head.

In entertainment news, the surprise TV hit is *The Osbournes,* in which viewers follow the wacky antics of zonked-out rocker Ozzy Osbourne, played, in the performance of his career, by David Hasselhoff.

In the Academy Awards, the Oscar for best picture goes to *A Beautiful Mind,* the uplifting story of legendary mathematical genius John Nash, who received a Nobel Prize decades after his descent into insanity, caused by attempting to do his own income taxes. On the music front, the U.S. recording industry is buoyed by a report that fourteen-year-old Jason Plempitt of Knoxville, Tenn., went into a music store and actually purchased a CD, making him the first teenager in three years to pay money for a recording rather than download it for free from the Internet. The humiliated youngster quickly informs his classmates that his computer is broken.

On a sadder note, two beloved public figures pass away: Milton "Mr. Television" Berle, who was ninety-three, and Britain's Queen Mother Elizabeth, who was 247. They are laid to rest in identical dresses.

But there is little rest to be had in . . .

APRIL

. . . when Secretary of State Colin Powell travels to the Middle East to (1) restore peace to the troubled region and (2) receive a plaque from the Association of Troubled Middle East Travel Agencies honoring him for making the five-thousandth official U.S. peacekeeping trip. At the awards ceremony, Powell jokes: "We expect to get this thing resolved any day now," which gets a big laugh, punctuated by mortar fire. On Powell's arrival back in Washington, President Bush hails the trip as "a major success," noting that the secretary of state brought home "much of his original luggage." The stock market drops 518 points.

In France, the first round of the presidential elections produces alarming evidence of a right-wing resurgence in the country when the second-place vote getter, finishing just behind incumbent Jacques Chirac, is Pat Buchanan.

In other international news, a euphoric Argentina president Eduardo Duhalde announces that he has received an e-mail stating that Argentina can make a surefire $500 million via a foolproof plan. All Argentina has to do is send $10 million to the top name on the e-mail list, which is . . . Iraq.

On the domestic terrorism front, the U.S. Immigration and Naturalization Service, tightening up its procedures, quietly reverses its decision to grant a student visa to Osama bin Laden. This decisive action enables the Department of Homeland Insecurity to ratchet the nation's Color Code Security Status all the way down to Mauve ("Calm But Tense").

Things are not so peaceful, however, in professional baseball, where a dispute between players and owners threatens to ruin the season and, with it, the social lives of thousands of fantasy baseball dweebs. At issue is what the players and owners can do to restore the goodwill and trust of pro baseball's increasingly alienated fans.

Ha-ha! No, really, the issue is how each side can snag the most possible money before the game goes completely into the toilet. The talks open on a tense note, as the owners' charges of steroid abuse are met with vehement denials by players'

union representatives, who quickly reduce a large oak conference table to kindling.

In cultural news, Oprah Winfrey announces that she is dis-
continuing her book club because she has run out of good ti-
tles to recommend to her audience, as evidenced by her final
selection, *Fifty Fun Celery Recipes.*

Lisa "Left Eye" Lopes hip-hops off the big stage.

And speaking of the entertainment industry, in . . .

MAY

. . . the big news is the release of the fifth installment in the
Star Wars series, *Star Wars II,* which continues to express
creator/director George Lucas's artistic vision, summed up by
the statement: "I don't understand Roman numerals." The
movie seems to be an effort by Lucas to connect with younger
audiences, as evidenced by the exciting action scene in which

Anakin Skywalker battles the evil Count Dooku in a deadly high-stakes game of Quidditch.

In other film news, al-Qaeda, apparently seeking to disprove reports that its leader is dead, releases its latest video, *The Osama bin Laden Fugitive Workout.* The Department of Homeland Insecurity decides to ratchet the nation's Color Code Security Status up a notch to Key Lime ("Partly Cloudy").

In other War on Terrorism developments, the Federal Transportation Security Administration opposes a proposal to let airline pilots carry guns, the official reasoning being that, hey, what if terrorists got on the plane and in their struggle to kill the pilots so they could take control of the cockpit and fly the plane into a building and kill a lot more people a pilot fired his gun at them but missed? Somebody could get hurt!

On the international front, President Bush and Russian president Vladimir Putin sign an arms reduction treaty under which the U.S. will destroy about two-thirds of its nuclear arsenal and Russia will "make every effort, within reason," to try to find out who, exactly, HAS its nuclear arsenal.

America observes Mother's Day in traditional fashion, with an estimated 125 million families taking their moms to dinner at an estimated three restaurants.

In economic news, Merrill Lynch agrees to pay a $100 million fine for luring naïve investors into buying stocks in risky Internet companies. The firm will raise this money by luring naïve investors into buying stocks in companies that have not yet tanked. The market responds by dropping 1,247 points.

In South Florida, efforts to create a new artificial reef out of the decommissioned navy ship *Spiegel Grove* go awry when the 510-foot vessel, instead of sinking as planned, is elected lieutenant governor. It's "back to the drawing board" for the state's beleaguered elections officials.

In entertainment news, the surprise hit TV "reality show" of the spring is *India and Pakistan Threaten to Start a Nuclear War.* But after a few weeks of waiting for something to happen, viewers become bored and go back to watching the perennial ratings favorite, *Amateur Video of Police Officers Beating Up a Motorist.*

In sports action, the World Cup gets under way with defending champion France playing Senegal—a lowly underdog and former French colony—in an exciting match that ends in a stunning upset win by . . . Iraq.

Sam Snead finally reaches the 19th hole.

And speaking of icons, in . . .

JUNE

. . . Britain's Queen Elizabeth II celebrates the fiftieth year of her reign at a star-studded gala concert featuring performances by Paul McCartney, Phil Collins, Eric Clapton, and

Ozzy Osbourne, who, in the dramatic highlight of the evening, bites the head off one of the Queen's Welsh corgis.

But the mood is not so jubilant in the Middle East, where, following a series of Palestinian attacks, Israeli tanks again surround the headquarters of Yasser Arafat and slowly press against it until it is the size of a twin bed. The crafty Arafat escapes again by claiming he has a dental appointment.

Speaking of close calls: On June 14, a giant asteroid, discovered only three days earlier, passes within seventy-five thousand miles of Earth. Congress immediately holds hearings, with the Democrats charging that the Bush administration should have known about it sooner and the Republicans noting that the asteroid had been heading this way during all eight years of the Clinton administration. The CIA acknowledges, under questioning, that at one point it was tracking the asteroid but lost the file. In the end, all parties agree that airport security needs to be tightened.

In another alarming story, wildfires rage out of control in Colorado and several other western states, burning thousands of acres and destroying dozens of homes. Investigators searching an area where one of the largest blazes originated find a Zippo lighter bearing a thumbprint belonging to . . . Iraq.

The nation's Color Code Security Status is quickly raised to Maroon ("Dark Brownish Red").

On Wall Street, the bad news continues. First, WorldCom announces that it has improperly accounted for $3.9 billion and has "at least six" movies seriously overdue for return to Blockbuster. Next, Xerox, under pressure from investigators, admits that its second-quarter profits were actually a copy of its first-quarter profits. Next, Martha Stewart is linked to a string of bank robberies. The stock market drops 11,600 points.

Ann Landers dies but continues to dispense common-sense advice.

In legal news, a Dayton, Ohio, jury, in a unanimous verdict, orders five cigarette companies to pay $128 billion to a sixty-seven-year-old man, despite the fact that the man (1) is not a smoker, (2) has not sued anybody, and (3) is in fact on trial for littering. The Association of Trial Lawyers of America hails this as "a major victory for our Porsche dealership." In California, a federal appeals court rules that schools cannot compel American schoolchildren to say the Pledge of Allegiance, on the grounds that "allegiance" has too many syllables.

And speaking of legal trouble, in . . .

JULY

. . . two pilots scheduled to fly an America West plane from Miami to Phoenix are ordered from the cockpit at Miami International Airport and found to be drunk. The pilots aroused suspicions when they made a preflight announcement asking if any passenger "happens to have a corkscrew."

In international news, the United Nations Security Council, finally taking action against a scourge that has plagued humanity for decades, unanimously passes a resolution authorizing member nations to "feel free to shoot down the next bored billionaire who tries to fly around the world in a balloon."

In financial news, Congress, addressing the corporate accounting scandals, approves the death penalty for anybody convicted of exercising a stock option. As the market plunges 128,500 points, Federal Reserve Board chairman Alan Greenspan, in a move that fails to bolster investor confidence, announces that from now on he wants to be paid in gold.

In sports, baseball immortal Ted Williams dies. His son says the body will be frozen so it can be revived in the future. A court approves this plan, on the condition that the son be frozen at the same time so he can be revived in the future to explain everything to his dad. We wish.

In other science news, archaeologists announce that they have discovered a skull that is believed to be more than six million years old. Tests show that the skull does, indeed, belong to Sen. Strom Thurmond.

In political news, the U.S. House of Representatives votes to expel Rep. James Traficant (D-*Sopranos*) after a House Ethics Committee investigation shows that the thing on his head is a diseased weasel that has eaten nearly 80 percent of his brain. The vote to expel him is 420 to 1, with the lone dissenting vote coming from . . . Iraq.

Speaking of victims, Michael Jackson tells a New York rally that—we are not making this up—he has been oppressed by his record label. Concerned fans from around the world send donations of money, food, sequins, and facial implants.

But a month of bad news ends on an upbeat note when rescuers break through to a collapsed Pennsylvania mine shaft and free nine miners who have been trapped 240 feet underground for more than three days. Also rescued are 157 lawyers who have burrowed down there to offer their services in the filing of lawsuits.

Speaking of money, in . . .

AUGUST

. . . financially strapped Brazil, in a cash-raising move considered by some experts in international law to be of questionable legality, announces that it has sold Uruguay to Paraguay for $200 million.

On the domestic front, the economic news continues to be bad, with these alarming developments:

- The Council of Business Economists releases a study concluding that the U.S. economy will continue to worsen "as long as AT&T keeps running those commercials with Carrot Top."

- Airline industry losses continue to mount, forcing America West, in a cost-cutting measure, to eliminate the cockpit minibar.
- WorldCom executives admit to investigators that, in a clear deviation from accepted business accounting standards and practices, they heated their headquarters by burning money.
- As the stock market plunges 1.2 million points, President Bush makes a speech urging Americans to "have faith in our economy," adding: "Thank God that I, personally, am guaranteed a generous pension."

On a brighter note, the owners and players of Major League Baseball agree, in a heartwarming display of cooperation and concern for the National Pastime, to continue raking in money. Commissioner Bud Selig announces that, in an effort to win back the trust of disillusioned fans, "We're going to fix it so Anaheim wins the Series."

Lionel Hampton is gone, but his vibes ring on.

On the history front, divers seeking to recover the gun turret of the USS *Monitor* on the ocean floor off the coast of North Carolina discover surprising evidence that the Civil War gunship was sunk by . . . Iraq. The nation's Color Code Security Status is raised to Peach ("Viewer Discretion Advised").

And speaking of fugitives: Martha Stewart, pursued by the

Securities and Exchange Commission, flees to a remote area of Westport, Conn., and barricades herself inside a primitive cabin with only nine bathrooms. SEC agents surround the structure but are reluctant to attack, as Stewart is known to possess a set of very sharp paring knives and a military-grade glue gun. "She can't hold out forever," states one agent. "We believe she has only a three-day supply of fennel."

But things get even scarier in . . .

SEPTEMBER

. . . when Florida, having learned nothing from history, attempts to hold another election. Everything goes smoothly, with virtually no problems reported—until the polls open. Then there is chaos, especially in Broward and Miami-Dade Counties, which are using new computerized voting machines. Election officials begin to suspect that the system might have been programmed incorrectly when, instead of reporting the vote totals, the machines connect to the Internet and send out 126 million e-mails offering discount Viagra.

In other Florida news, police shut down I-75 for hours and arrest three men of Middle Eastern descent after a woman reports that she overheard them in a Shoney's Restaurant talking about what she believed to be a terrorist plot. It turns out to be a misunderstanding: The men are medical students.

Responding quickly, the Department of Homeland Insecurity orders all 350 Shoney's to install metal detectors.

Robert Torricelli announces that he is dropping out of the New Jersey Senate race because he is a good man who has done nothing wrong. The state Democratic Party, looking for a "name" to replace him on the ballot, decides, in a move of questionable legality, to go with "John F. Kennedy."

U.S. news organizations observe the anniversary of the Sept. 11 attacks with investigative reports about the nation's continued vulnerability to terrorism. First, the New York *Daily News* reports that two of its reporters carried box cutters, razor knives, and pepper spray on fourteen commercial flights without getting caught. Then ABC News reports that it smuggled fifteen pounds of uranium into New York City. Then Fox News reports that it flew Osama bin Laden to Washington, D.C., and videotaped him touring the White House. The nation's Color Code Security Status is ratcheted up to its third-highest level, Burnt Umber ("Medium Rare").

On the medical front, an outbreak of the deadly West Nile virus prompts six states to enact strict laws requiring the registration of mosquitoes. It does not go unnoticed by the Bush administration that the West Nile is probably in the same general area as . . . Iraq.

In entertainment news, the coveted Emmy for best TV drama goes to the new hit show, *Mall Parking Lot Surveillance Video of Woman Belting Her Child,* which is running on all major networks twenty-four hours a day to guard against the danger that somebody, somewhere, might have missed it. The grand prize in the phenomenally popular talent-search show *American Idol* is won by perky female singer Kelly Clarkson, played, in the performance of his career, by David Hasselhoff.

In financial news, agents of the Securities and Exchange Commission stage a predawn attack on the Martha Stewart cabin only to discover that the domestic diva has escaped through a six-hundred-yard tunnel, which she apparently dug by hand using a heart-shaped dessert scoop (stainless steel, dishwasher safe, $38 at marthastewart.com). The stock market falls to minus infinity, its lowest level in nearly two weeks.

But the bad news only gets worse in . . .

OCTOBER

. . . when the Washington, D.C., area is terrorized by a string of deadly sniper attacks. After weeks of escalating fear and tension, police are finally able to break the case by identifying, then arresting, the only two males in the United States who have not appeared on CNN or Fox as sniper experts.

Speaking of terror: Saddam Hussein, having campaigned under the catchy populist slogan "A Vote for Saddam Is a Vote for Not Getting Both Your Feet Chopped Off Without Anesthetic," is reelected with a solid 127 percent of the popular vote, which includes several thousand votes apparently cast via Internet from Broward and Miami-Dade Counties.

Another closely watched election is held in Brazil, where the voters—in a move sure to inspire confidence in the international financial community—elect, as their new president, a man named "Lula." The economic news is not so good in the United States, where the New York Stock Exchange, in what is seen by many analysts as a troubling sign, announces that it will henceforth be operating out of a pushcart in Battery Park.

But the scariest news comes from North Korea, which announces that, in violation of a 1994 agreement with the United States, it is developing nuclear weapons. An angry President Bush responds by pointing out that "if you spell

NEW HOME
OF
NEW YORK
STOCK
EXCHANGE

KOREA backward, you get AEROK, which sounds a heck of a lot like . . . Iraq." Reacting quickly, the Department of Homeland Insecurity produces, in mere hours, a new Color Code Security Status: Tangerine ("UH-oh!").

In politics, a tragic plane crash claims the life of Sen. Paul Wellstone of Minnesota, whose loss is mourned at a memorial service featuring rousing eulogies and music by Limp Bizkit. The state's Democratic Party, looking for a replacement with name recognition, taps Walter Mondale, who, after some prompting, is indeed able to recognize his name. In a speech accepting the nomination, Mondale confidently predicts that he will "send Mr. Reagan back to California."

In the feel-good sports story of the year, the plucky and spunky Anaheim Angels, in what almost seems like a scripted outcome, defeat the San Francisco Barry Bonds in a nail-biter of a World Series that captivates millions of viewers, including several dozen living outside of California.

And speaking of contests, in . . .

NOVEMBER

. . . the Republicans win big in the midterm elections, giving President Bush a clear mandate to push forward with his foreign and domestic agendas, as soon as he thinks a domestic agenda up. In a somber postelection speech, the president reaffirms his solemn commitment, no matter how long it takes, to learn to pronounce "nuclear." The Democrats, desperate for leadership and beginning to realize that Walter Mondale is not the answer, begin making discreet inquiries into the availability of Hubert Humphrey. In Florida, the computerized voting goes surprisingly smoothly, with election officials reporting no major "glitches," and a strong turnout of eighty-seven trillion voters.

Al Gore emerges from his Resting Pod to let everyone know that he is not at ALL bitter about the fact that he was TOTALLY ripped off in 2000 and really should be the president, and is WAY smarter than George W., not to mention that Tipper is WAY more of a babe than Laura. The former vice president declares that he has not decided whether he will run for president again; he mulls this difficult question over in a series of heartfelt self-probing appearances on *Meet the Press, Larry King Live, The Today Show, The Tonight Show with Jay Leno, Late Night with David Letterman, Monday Night Football, Emeril Live, The Simpsons,* and *The Victoria's Secret Fashion Show,* where Gore expresses his belief that the dominant issue of the twenty-first century will be biodegradable underwear.

World tension eases when Iraqi dictator Saddam Hussein, under intense international pressure, announces that he will allow UN weapons inspectors "full access to Ahvaz, Hamedan, Mashad, Rasht, Urmiya, and Zahedan." World tension increases again when the UN inspectors, having visited these sites, report that they are located in Iran.

Elsewhere in the War on Terrorism, Osama bin Laden, apparently concerned that he has been overshadowed in recent months by other world personalities, releases a new audiotape in which he states that he is "available for meetings, parties, weddings, and corporate functions." In Yemen, a vehicle carrying a top al-Qaeda leader is vaporized by a Hellfire missile fired by an unmanned U.S. drone plane. Many Americans ask the obvious question: If we have this technology, why haven't we used it on . . . Geraldo?

In entertainment news, nearly thirty million viewers tune in to watch the finale of *The Bachelor,* in which banker Aaron Buerge chooses, as his bride-to-be, psychologist Helene Eksterowicz, much to the dismay of the popular favorite runner-up, David Hasselhoff. Michael Jackson takes time out from his busy schedule of being an oppressed humanitarian to demonstrate the correct method for displaying an infant to a crowd from a fifth-floor balcony. Actress Winona Ryder is convicted of shoplifting, surprising CNN and Fox shoplifting experts who had been predicting for weeks that she would be a white male loner.

In an ominous development, SEC agents confirm reports that Martha Stewart recently contracted with a leading New York architectural firm to design her a cave. The Color Code Security is quickly bumped up to Jalapeño ("Everyone DOWN!").

Speaking of scary situations, in . . .

DECEMBER

. . . hopes for peace soar when Saddam Hussein, as ordered by the UN, finally turns over a list of materials that could be used to make weapons of mass destruction. These hopes are dashed when UN inspectors begin translating the list from Arabic and find that the first item is "a partridge in a pear tree."

Not to be outshone on the international stage, Osama bin Laden issues a press release stating that he is involved in "seri-

ous negotiations" with a "major studio" for "an important role in *Jackass 2*."

On the economic front, a group of troubled U.S. airlines, faced with overwhelming losses, announces that in an effort to cut fuel costs their pilots will periodically turn off the engines during flight and coast for what an airline spokesperson describes as "a reasonable distance." The spokesperson stresses that this procedure "is perfectly safe" and will be used "only over soft terrain."

In another troubling story, a new medical study shows that Americans are not only fat but they are also starting to give off what researchers describe as "a really bad smell."

In a surprise political development, Al Gore, having apparently received a status report from Earth, announces that he will not run for president in 2004. Within hours, the Democratic Party leadership, reacting to this devastating news, runs out of champagne. On the Republican side, Sen. Trent Lott gets himself into hot water when the news media report that (1) he suggested Strom Thurmond would be a good president, and (2) his DNA is virtually identical to that of a mackerel.

Congress, in a widely hailed and long-overdue effort to control the worsening celebrity glut, passes a law requiring that when a TV show such as *American Idol* creates a star, at least one existing star must be deported. Within hours, the Backstreet Boys are on an Air Force transport bound for Uzbekistan.

But the news is not so good from a remote, forbidding mountain region near Westport, Conn., where SEC agents prepare to attack a centrally heated, 24,500-square-foot, Country French–style cave containing Martha Stewart only to discover that their worst-case nightmare scenario has become a reality: The fugitive taste goddess has gotten hold of a nuclear food processor. "If she presses the POWER button," states one official, "New England is radioactive coleslaw." In response, the Color Code Security Status is ratcheted up to its highest level, Traffic Cone Orange ("Yikes!").

And thus the year ends on a somewhat disturbing note. But this does not prevent the nation from pausing, on the eve of 2003, to gather with friends, to drink champagne, to blow into cardboard horns, to sing "Auld Lang Syne," to reflect on the year gone past, and, above all, to realize, a little too late, that those cardboard horns are manufactured abroad and would make a perfect vehicle for spreading chemical or biological warfare agents.

But Happy New Year, anyway.

2003

ANYBODY SEEN ANY WMD?

I t was the Year of the Troubling Question.

The most troubling one was: What the heck happened to all those weapons of mass destruction that were supposed to be in Iraq? Apparently, there was an intelligence mix-up. As CIA director George Tenet noted recently, "Our thinking now is that the weapons of mass destruction might actually be in that other one, whaddycallit, Iran. Or Michigan. We're pretty sure the letter *i* is involved."

Some other troubling questions from 2003 were:

- If Californians hated Gray Davis so much, why did they elect him governor TWICE? Did Gray have photos of the entire California electorate naked? Can we see them?

- Why did Jennifer Lopez and Ben Affleck—whose sole achievement in 2003 was to costar in *Gigli,* a film so bad it was used to torture suspected terrorists—receive more media attention than the entire continent of Asia, and nearly as much as Kobe Bryant?

- Who's watching all these "reality" TV shows? Nobody admits to watching them. Everybody agrees they're even stupider than those infomercials wherein Ron Popeil spends thirty minutes liquefying vegetables to the rapturous delight of a live, if half-witted, audience. And yet "reality" shows keep getting ratings. Who are the viewers? Have houseplants learned to operate remote controls?

- Can young people wear their pants any lower? Their waistbands are now at approximately knee level. Where will this trend end? The shins? The feet? Will young people eventually detach themselves from their pants altogether and just drag them along behind, connected to their ankles by a belt?

We don't know the answers to any of these questions. All we know is that 2003 is finally, we hope, over. But before we move on, let's put our heads between our knees and take one last look back at this remarkable year, which started, as is so often the case, with . . .

JANUARY

... which begins with traditional New Year's Day celebrations all over the world, except at the Central Intelligence Agency, which, acting on what it believes to be accurate information, observes Thanksgiving.

In college football, the University of Miami Hurricanes defeat Ohio State in the Fiesta Bowl and reign as national champions for roughly a week, at the end of which a Fiesta Bowl official—a man with the reaction time of a Sequoia who has been standing in the end zone the whole time reflecting on the final play—throws a penalty flag, thus giving the game to Ohio State in what future legal scholars will deem the most flagrant miscarriage of justice in human history. Not that we Miami fans are still bitter.

On a brighter note, President Bush announces a plan to boost the sagging United States economy via a two-pronged stimulus package consisting of (1) visiting Crawford, Tex., and (2) prayer.

Meanwhile, a claim by the Raelians, a UFO cult, that they have produced a human clone baby named Eve is increasingly viewed with skepticism by scientists. "Having looked at their so-called evidence," state the scientists, "we strongly suspect that the clone baby is actually named Rachel."

In medical news, researchers studying heart attack victims announce that a person who drinks a glass or two of wine or beer is, quote, "significantly more likely to do the Macarena."

World tension mounts when North Korea announces that it is withdrawing from the nuclear nonproliferation treaty on the grounds that it's really hard to pronounce "proliferation." Faced with clear-cut evidence that the North Koreans are actively developing weapons of mass destruction, President Bush vows to determine whether North Korea "is located anywhere near Iraq."

In politics, Rep. Harold Farnwimble of Ohio becomes the only Democratic member of Congress to formally declare that he is not running for president. He immediately surges ahead in the polls.

On the technological front, a fast-spreading "worm" virus cripples Internet e-mail traffic, briefly bringing the international penis-enlargement industry to . . . well, to its knees.

In pro football, the Tampa Bay Buccaneers defeat the heavily favored Oakland Raiders and win the Super Bowl, despite the objections of Fiesta Bowl officials who want to award the victory to Ohio State.

Speaking of setbacks, in . . .

FEBRUARY

. . . United States coalition-building efforts are dealt a severe blow when France announces that it will not participate in the impending Iraq invasion, a decision that, in the words of

Defense Secretary Donald Rumsfeld, "could seriously impair our ability to surrender."

American citizens show their disdain for all things French by boycotting French wine, calling French fries "freedom fries," and taking showers.

Elsewhere in the War on Terror, the Department of Homeland Security urges Americans to stock up on food, water, flashlights, duct tape, and plastic sheeting. Within hours, al-Qaeda surrenders, stating: "We cannot fight flashlights AND duct tape."

Meanwhile, tension between the United States and North Korea continues to mount as North Korea, in what the White House calls "a deliberate act of provocation," uses nuclear missiles to destroy Columbus, Ohio. A visibly angry President Bush warns the North Koreans that they "better not give any of those missiles to Iraq."

On the economic front, the struggling airline industry undergoes another round of cost cutting, highlighted by United Airlines' announcement that, beginning in March, passengers on international flights "will have to eat each other."

On Valentine's Day, millions of men give millions of women flowers, cards, and candy as a heartfelt expression of the emotion that also motivates men to observe anniversaries and birthdays: fear.

In entertainment news, Rachel the imaginary UFO cult baby is signed to do a "reality" TV show. In yet another indication of the nation's worsening obesity crisis, a new medical study concludes that Americans are now so fat that "they are causing tides."

Late in the month, a massive "Storm of the Century" blizzard batters the Northeast with icy blasts and holds the region in its wintry grip, blanketing New England with white stuff, as emergency crews struggle to keep the news media supplied with weather clichés.

And things only get worse in . . .

MARCH

. . . when North Korean troops invade Oregon, prompting a grim-faced President Bush to declare that "time is running out for the Iraqi regime." But the United States continues to have trouble getting other nations to join the coalition and is forced to bribe Turkey by giving the Turkish government an "economic aid package" consisting of $37 billion in cash, plus unlimited nighttime and weekend minutes, plus what is described as a "hard-to-get video" of Britney Spears. With Turkey on board, the coalition now consists of seven nations, assuming you count Guam, Puerto Rico, and Staten Island as nations.

As it becomes clear that an Iraqi invasion is imminent and war is at hand, Democrats in Congress, setting aside partisan politics, pledge "total, unwavering, and unconditional support" for the president and commander in chief "unless anything bad happens."

While all this is going on, Osama bin Laden attempts to surrender to U.S. authorities but is told to come back later, everybody is busy.

Meanwhile, Saddam Hussein, in a last-ditch effort to stay in power, declares that he has been the victim of "identity theft," and somebody else, using his name and Social Security number, has actually been running Iraq for the past two decades. In response, the United Nations Security Council, meeting in emergency session, votes 15 to 0 to continue patronizing expensive Manhattan restaurants.

But it is too little, too late. On March 19, coalition forces attack Iraq; within days, they control most of the southern part of the country and have taken many prisoners, including two of the three known Dixie Chicks. They do not immediately uncover any weapons of mass destruction, but they do find a warehouse containing a large quantity of what is believed to be refined sugar, which CIA intelligence analysts note "is a leading cause of tooth decay."

In nonwar news:

- An outbreak of the SARS virus in Asia is blamed for dozens of deaths, many of them travel agents committing suicide.

⚬ The Academy Awards are held, with the Oscar for Best Picture going to *Chicago,* only to be taken away by a Fiesta Bowl official and awarded to Ohio State.

And speaking of drama, in . . .

APRIL

. . . coalition forces capture Baghdad, and hopes soar for a quick resolution to the conflict when a cheering Iraqi crowd topples a huge statue of Saddam. But these hopes are quickly dashed when, tragically, the statue fails to land on Geraldo. Saddam himself is nowhere to be found, though he does release a videotape announcing plans to take his career "in a new direction," possibly including a "reality" TV show called *Queer Eye for a Dictator Guy,* in which he will undergo a makeover by five gay men, who will then be executed.

On the weapons of mass destruction front, coalition troops discover three barrels of lard, described by U.S. intelligence sources as "a heart attack waiting to happen."

As the war grinds on, some welcome moments of comic relief are provided by the Iraqi information minister, Mohammed Saeed al-Sahhaf, who becomes an international laughingstock by continuing to insist, despite overwhelming evidence, that the Americans are being routed. He is quickly hired as a Fiesta Bowl official.

In other news:

- The Masters Golf Tournament goes smoothly despite a mass protest by an estimated four people against Augusta National's membership policy, defended by a person named "Hootie," of accepting only deceased males. "Someday, we may decide to accept women," Hootie says, "but only if they are males."
- *The New York Times* suffers a credibility crisis when numerous stories by reporter Jayson Blair are found to contain inaccuracies, such as the assertion, in a story about the D.C.-area sniper case, that the sun is carried across the sky by a giant turtle. ("In fact," notes the

Times, "it is the moon.") Blair, thoroughly disgraced, is forced to accept a six-figure book contract.

○ American Airlines, in a move to cut labor costs, replaces some pilots with baggage handlers, but stresses that this change applies "only to daytime flights."

○ North Korean troops capture Wisconsin.

But things brighten a bit in . . .

MAY

. . . when President Bush lands on the aircraft carrier USS *Abraham Lincoln* off the coast of California and declares to a crowd of sailors that major combat has ended. The jubilation is dampened somewhat when, moments after the president's plane departs, the carrier is severely damaged by a car bomb.

Meanwhile, in Iraq itself, looting continues to be a problem, as dramatized by the discovery that both the Tigris and Euphrates Rivers are missing. On a more positive note, efforts to establish a Western-style democracy in Iraq move forward with the arrival, as consultants, of Florida election officials. Within hours, the nation plunges back into chaos.

Elsewhere abroad, Chinese health authorities, stung by accusations that they have been slow in reacting to the SARS virus, announce that they will execute anybody who gets sick.

In domestic news, Congress enacts massive tax cuts in an effort to, in the words of a Republican leader, "see if we can push the deficit over the skillion-dollar mark." The major Democratic presidential candidates denounce the cuts and vow to repeal them, because promising to increase taxes is a proven vote winner on the planet they come from, namely, Planet Walter Mondale.

Florida becomes the latest state to ban smoking in restaurants. California, determined to stay ahead of the trend, bans eating in restaurants.

In an inspiring story of courage, hiker Aron Ralston, trapped in a remote Utah canyon, frees himself by amputating his own right arm. Somehow he manages to fashion a tourniquet and hike back to civilization, where he is slapped with a $17 million negligence lawsuit by lawyers representing the arm.

North Korean troops occupy the Washington Monument.

In sports, golfer Annika Sorenstam competes in a PGA tournament, setting off a major round of diaper changing among the membership of Augusta National. Meanwhile, Nike signs a $90 million endorsement deal with eighteen-year-old basketball player and Humvee owner LeBron James Incorporated. To pay for this, Nike raises the average price of a pair of its sneakers to $385, which includes $1.52 for materials and 17 cents for labor.

In yet another sign of declining national educational standards, a twelve-year-old Vermont girl wins the National

Spelling Bee in Washington by spelling "horse." She actually spells it "h-o-r-s," but the judges rule that this is "close enough."

In entertainment news, CNN switches to a new format that consists entirely of Larry King talking to former prosecutors about Laci Peterson.

Speaking of upbeat, in . . .

JUNE

. . . hopes for peace in the Mideast soar when President Bush meets with Israeli and Palestinian leaders in a landmark summit, which goes really well until gunfire erupts over the seating arrangements.

Meanwhile, a political controversy brews over a little-noticed statement in the president's January State of the Union address, in which he asserted that Iraq, under Saddam Hussein, was "located right next to Connecticut." The CIA heatedly denies responsibility for the error, noting, "We clearly said Delaware."

On the crime front, Martha Stewart is indicted on charges of securities fraud and obstruction of justice. "Also," states a federal prosecutor, "we believe that some of her casseroles contained human body parts."

Speaking of unhealthy: An outbreak of monkeypox (really)

forces federal authorities to ban the sale of, among other animals, Gambian giant pouched rats. It is not immediately clear why anybody would want a giant pouched rat or why such a person would not deserve to get a disease.

In sports, the University of Miami confirms reports that it is thinking about leaving the Big East athletic conference for the National Football League.

On the literary front, the blockbuster bestseller of the year is the long-awaited fifth Harry Potter book, *Harry Potter Reaches Puberty and Starts Taking Really Long Showers.* Another hot seller is Sen. Hillary Clinton's new book, *I Can't Help It If I'm a Saint,* in which, with great candor and openness, her ghostwriter reveals the most intimate details of Sen. Clinton's life, except the parts that might be interesting, which fall within Sen. Clinton's "Zone of Privacy." Promoting her book on a nationwide, multicity "Zone of Privacy Tour," Sen. Clinton repeatedly denies that she plans to run for president, insisting that she is totally dedicated to "representing my constituents in, you know, that state."

North Korean troops, growing desperate for attention, announce plans to appear in a new "reality" TV show, tentatively titled *We Have Conquered Your Nation, Capitalist Scum,* but it is canceled when network executives find out that nobody involved is blond.

The downward spiral continues in . . .

JULY

. . . when President Bush goes to Africa for a five-day visit that goes quite well, considering the fact that the president, relying on U.S. intelligence reports, is under the impression he is touring Switzerland. Once the confusion is straightened out, the president has what the White House describes as a "very constructive meeting" with "a very influential group" of elephants.

Meanwhile, hopes for democracy dim in Iraq when the postwar governing council of Iraqi leaders, holding its first meeting, votes to hire James Carville. On a positive note, U.S. forces kill Odai and Qusai Hussein, who are immediately signed to appear on a "reality" TV show called *Who Wants to Take a Gander at the Bodies of Two Slimeball Dictator's Sons.*

In the Caribbean, the U.S. Coast Guard intercepts a group of Cubans attempting to travel from Cuba to Florida in a 1951 Chevrolet pickup truck. The Coast Guard arrests the Cubans and sinks the truck after a computer check shows that it has an expired registration. "Also," states the Coast Guard, "they were not signaling lane changes."

Domestically, the big news is in California, where—in a catastrophe long predicted by geologists—a massive, violent tectonic shift opens a huge fault in the Earth's crust, releasing a vast mutant swarming horde of gubernatorial candidates. "It's terrible!" reports one rescue worker. "There's porn stars, washed-up actors, strippers, fanatics, lunatics, and somebody named Cruz Bustamante." Federal troops are ordered into the state, where they immediately become stuck in traffic.

Disney World, in what turns out to be a hugely successful promotion, holds the first-ever "North Korean Troops Day."

In sports, Lance Armstrong wins a record-tying fifth Tour de France and celebrates, as is traditional, by having his bicycle seat surgically removed from his butt.

In entertainment news, CNN, concerned about flagging viewer interest in the Laci Peterson format, switches to "All Kobe, All the Time." The music industry, in what is seen as a last-ditch effort to halt the sharing of music files on the Internet, asks a federal judge to issue an injunction against "the possession or use of electricity."

Speaking of which, the big domestic story in . . .

AUGUST

. . . begins on a quiet weekday morning in rural northern Ohio where eighty-three-year-old widow Eileen Freemonkle decides that, for a change, she will put two Pop-Tarts into her toaster instead of her usual one. This rogue action—never anticipated by the designers of the nation's electrical power grid—sets off a chain of events that ultimately blacks out the entire Northeast. As rescue crews work overtime trying to keep people in the affected areas supplied with news about the

developing Kobe Bryant situation, Congress swings into emergency action. Within hours, Democrats and Republicans have issued literally hundreds of press releases blaming each other. Power is finally restored several days later by power company workers, aided by bored North Korean troops.

In Iraq, United States troops capture a cousin of Saddam Hussein known as "Chemical Ali"; a search of his person fails to uncover any weapons of mass destruction, but he is carrying a Bic pen that, as CIA analysts are quick to note, "could poke out somebody's eye."

Mars makes its closest approach to Earth in human history, prompting Arnold Schwarzenegger to declare, to Jay Leno, that he is running for governor of California. In other political news, Howard Dean emerges as the leading Democratic presidential candidate thanks to a novel Internet fund-raising strategy in which he pretends to be a wealthy Nigerian businessman.

In a controversial ruling, the Alabama Supreme Court orders a monument depicting the Ten Commandments removed from the judicial building after an audit shows that it actually has fourteen commandments, including two that say "Roll Tide!" In other religious news, Episcopal church leaders, in a highly controversial decision following bitter debate, confirm the church's first openly Jewish bishop.

In the arts, Madonna, demonstrating the courage, creativity, and talent that have made her name synonymous with the word "Madonna," kisses Britney Spears. This results in a worldwide tidal wave of publicity, followed by the emergence, on both performers, of lip sores.

And speaking of alarming, in . . .

SEPTEMBER

. . . Palestinian and Israeli leaders finally recover the Road Map to Peace, only to discover that, while they were looking for it, the Lug Nuts of Mutual Interest came off the Front Left Wheel of Accommodation, causing the Sport Utility Vehicle of Progress to crash into the Ditch of Despair.

Meanwhile, President Bush goes before the United Nations General Assembly to ask for help in rebuilding Iraq. After enjoying a hearty international laugh, everyone adjourns for dinner at upscale Manhattan restaurants.

In domestic politics, Gen. Wesley Clark joins the crowded field of Democratic contenders and declares that, if he is elected president, his first official act would be "to actually register as a Democrat." In other political news, the California governor's race is temporarily thrown into disarray when residents of the other forty-nine states file a class action lawsuit demanding the right to vote in the recall election on the grounds that "it's on TV all the time."

But the hot political news is a huge scandal that erupts in Washington after conservative columnist Robert Novak writes a column in which he reveals that the wife of a guy who was critical of the Bush administration's Iraqi policy and went to Africa on a fact-finding mission is in fact a CIA agent (the wife is, we mean), which he (Novak) allegedly was improperly told by a high-level White House source, who some people allege is Karl Rove, although he (Rove), also Novak, heatedly denies this, and if you think this scandal is incomprehensible you are in the vast human majority, but people in Washington are still so excited about it that they have to change their underwear hourly.

Meanwhile, Hurricane Isabel makes landfall on the Outer Banks of North Carolina, forcing the evacuation of twenty-three thousand North Korean troops.

In the War on Telemarketing, a federal judge in Oklahoma blocks the implementation of the federal Do Not Call list on the grounds that it is unconstitutional. Hours later, he reverses the ruling on the grounds that his house is surrounded by people with torches.

There is another popular uprising in . . .

OCTOBER

. . . when the people of California, by a large majority, vote to send incumbent governor Gray Davis back to his pod. They replace him with Arnold Schwarzenegger, who wins easily despite allegations that he gropes women, which he assures the voters that he will never do in his capacity as governor "without a really good reason." In his victory statement, Schwarzenegger announces that he will appoint a stunt governor, who will handle the tasks that he is physically unable to perform, such as pronouncing words.

In other California news, fires rage out of control in large sectors of the state, destroying hundreds of homes and an estimated twenty-seven thousand Starbucks.

In Washington, Congress approves President Bush's request for $87 billion to Iraqify Iraq so that it will be more Iraq-like. The money will also be used for the War on Terror, including $23.99 to pay for what is described as "a complete overhaul" of the U.S. intelligence community's Magic 8 Ball.

On the economic front, there is good news from the Commerce Department, which reports a sharp upturn in the nation's economy, credited primarily to spending by North Korean troops.

In the Democratic presidential race, Sen. Bob "Bob" Graham drops out of the presidential race, narrowing the Democratic field to 2,038 people if you count Dennis Kucinich.

In a surprising development, conservative radio-talk-show host Rush Limbaugh shocks his millions of listeners when, confirming tabloid reports, he reveals on his popular syndicated show that he is, biologically, a woman. He promises to get treatment.

In immigration news, federal agents in twenty-one states descend on Wal-Mart stores that are allegedly employing illegal immigrants. The agents emerge hours later, glassy-eyed, holding bags filled with hundreds of dollars' worth of bargains but unable to remember what they went in there for in the first place.

China, culminating a two-decade effort to develop a manned spaceflight program, puts its first astronaut in orbit. Work begins immediately on a program to develop a way to get him back down.

In health news, authorities in Boston, Chicago, and New York report a rash of suicide attempts after the Florida Marlins, a franchise with essentially the same amount of tradition as Britney Spears, win their second World Series in six years. The Marlins are helped by a fluke play in the National League play-offs when a foul ball, about to be caught by Cubs outfielder Moises Alou, is deflected by a man who is later identified as a Fiesta Bowl official.

And speaking of foul, in . . .

NOVEMBER

. . . a big political stink erupts over adding drug benefits to Medicare, with Republicans and Democrats battling fiercely to see who can pander the hardest to the crucial senior citizen voting bloc without letting the other voting blocs figure out how much they will have to pay. The Republicans prevail with the help of the AARP. This angers some AARP members, who attempt to burn their membership cards in protest but are unable to work those newfangled childproof cigarette lighters.

In other political news, Democratic front-runner Howard Dean creates a stir when he says he wants to be the candidate of "guys with Confederate flags in their pickup trucks." After harsh criticism from his 2,037 opponents, Dean clarifies his position, explaining that he meant "guys using their pickup trucks to take Confederate flags to the dump to burn them because Confederate flags are bad." This prompts his opponents to charge that burning flags could be environmentally harmful. In the end, the only thing everybody can agree on is that there should be some kind of expensive program for senior citizens who have Confederate flags.

In a move that outrages traditionalists, Massachusetts legalizes gay marriage. California, not to be outdone, outlaws marriage between heterosexuals.

In a dramatic Thanksgiving Day surprise, President Bush makes a top secret trip to Iraq, where he serves turkey to the troops and delivers a moving speech thanking them for their efforts. The visit puts the troops in high spirits until about three minutes after the president leaves, at which point the turkey, which turns out to be a "suicide turkey," explodes.

Elsewhere on the international front, a group of "trade ministers," whom nobody has ever heard of, gather in Miami to discuss something called the "FTAA," which nobody understands, while outside thousands of people protest for reasons that run the gamut from extremely vague to outright delusional. Most of the protestors are peaceful, although some become involved in violent clashes with North Korean troops. After a few days, everybody goes home and the whole thing seems like a weird dream.

In entertainment news, CBS cancels the made-for-TV movie *The Reagans* after conservatives object to the portrayal of Ronald Reagan, who is played in the movie by a heavily made-up Bette Midler. Similar charges are leveled against NBC for its movie about Jessica Lynch, who is forced to issue a statement stressing that, despite what the movie suggests, she had "nothing to do with raising the flag at Iwo Jima."

In other entertainment news, pop superstar Michael Jackson again finds himself in legal trouble when authorities in Santa Barbara order him fingerprinted and booked on charges of "extreme creepiness, even for California." Jackson's attorney expresses outrage, telling a press conference that his client "doesn't even HAVE fingerprints."

And the strangeness only gets stranger in . . .

DECEMBER

. . . which begins on an upbeat note thanks to strong holiday retail sales, as measured by the economic indicator of Mall Shoppers Injured in Fights Over Sony PlayStations. In other positive news, the Commerce Department reports that the economic recovery has finally resulted in job creation. "So far, it's only the one job, and it's in urinal maintenance," notes the department. "But if things work out, it could become full-time."

On the War on Terror front, the nation gets a chilling reminder of its continued vulnerability when more than two hundred federal airport security workers are hospitalized because of continued exposure to what medical investigators describe as "really funky passenger feet."

In a move that concerns legal scholars, the U.S. Supreme Court announces that it is switching to a new "reality" TV format, called *Who Wants to Be a Justice,* in which ordinary citizens will help the court decide cases. In its first decision, the court, by an 11 to 9 vote, raises the national speed limit to 140 miles per hour.

In other entertainment news, Madonna kisses Cher, Emeril, Paris Hilton, Barney, Flipper, and the Mormon Tabernacle Choir.

In a medical breakthrough, a Houston-based team of surgeons, working for seventeen hours in a risky, first-of-its-kind

operation, is able to separate a twenty-one-year-old woman from her cellular telephone. She expires within hours, but doctors report that the phone is stable, and they expect its condition to improve dramatically "once it finds a new host."

The month's biggest surprise occurs when U.S. troops finally capture a filthy and bedraggled Saddam Hussein hiding in a hole along with eleven other members of the cast of the CBS "reality" show *Survivor: Iraq*. The former dictator immediately hires attorney Johnnie Cochran, who reveals that his defense strategy will be based on the legal argument that "if there's no WMD, you must set him free."

The other big December surprise is another daring, hush-hush-secret holiday morale-building head-of-state visit, this one by North Korean leader Kim Jong Il, who secretly travels to Washington, D.C., where he holds a reception for occupying North Korean troops. The Department of Homeland Security, asked how Kim was able to enter the country undetected, speculates that "he must have removed his shoes."

Finally, in a heartwarming story of the season, on New Year's Eve U.S. military radar detects a mysterious object streaking across the sky. A telescopic investigation reveals that the object is what NASA describes as "a heavily modified" 1953 Ford pickup truck, driven by Cuban refugees, apparently bound for the Moon.

Here's hoping they make it. Here's also hoping that 2004 is a wonderful year, or at least better than 2003.

Which shouldn't be hard.

2004

THE POLITICS, THE PASSION, AND PARIS

Looking back on 2004, we have to conclude that it could have been worse.

"HOW?" you ask, spitting out your coffee.

Well, OK, a giant asteroid could have smashed into Earth and destroyed all human life except Paris Hilton and William Hung. Or Florida could have been hit by twenty hurricanes instead of just seventeen.

Or the Yankees could have won the World Series.

But no question, 2004 was bad. Consider:

○ We somehow managed to hold a presidential election campaign that for several months was devoted almost entirely to the burning issue of: Vietnam.

- Our Iraq policy, despite being discussed, debated, and agreed upon right up to the very highest levels of the White House, did not always seem to be wildly popular over there in Iraq.
- Osama bin Laden remained at large for yet another year (although we did manage, at long last, to put Martha Stewart behind bars).
- The federal budget deficit continued to worsen, despite the concerted effort of virtually every elected official in Washington—Republican or Democrat—to spend more money.
- As a nation, we managed somehow to get even fatter, despite the fact that anticarbohydrate mania worsened to the point where the average American would rather shoot heroin than eat a bagel.
- The "reality" show cancer continued to metastasize so that you couldn't turn on the TV without seeing either Donald Trump or a cavalcade of dimwits emoting dramatically about eating bugs, losing weight, marrying a millionaire, or remodeling a bathroom.
- Perhaps most alarming of all, Cher yet again extended her "farewell" tour, which began during the Jimmy Carter administration and is now expected to continue until the sun goes out.

So, all things considered, we're happy to be entering a new year, which, according to our calculations, will be 2005 (although the exit polls are predicting it will be 1997). But before we move on, let's swallow our antinausea medication and take one last look back at 2004, which began, as so many years seem to, with . . .

JANUARY

. . . a month that opens with all the magic, excitement, and glamour conjured up by the words "Iowa caucuses." All the political experts—having gauged the mood of the state by dining with each other at essentially three Des Moines restaurants—agree that the Democratic nomination has already been locked up by feisty yet irritable genius Vermont governor Howard Dean, thanks to his two unbeatable weapons: (1) the Internet and (2) college students wearing orange hats.

But it turns out that the Iowa voters, many of whom apparently do not eat at the right restaurants, are out of the loop regarding the Dean strategic brilliance. Instead they vote for John "I Served in Vietnam" Kerry, who served in Vietnam and also has many policies, although nobody, including him, seems to know for sure exactly what they are. Dean, reacting to his Iowa loss, gives an emotional concession speech that ends with him making a sound like a hog being castrated with a fondue fork. Incredibly, this fails to improve his poll standings.

Meanwhile, the Bush administration, increasingly disturbed

by the bad news from Iraq, cancels the White House's lone remaining subscription (*Baseball Digest*).

But the news is much better from Mars, where yet another spunky li'l NASA robot vehicle lands and begins transmitting back photographs of rocks that appear virtually identical to the rock photos beamed back by all the other spunky li'l NASA robots, thus confirming suspicions that the universe has a LOT of rocks in it. In other outer-space news, Michael Jackson, clearly concerned about his trial on charges of child molestation, dances on the roof of an SUV.

In lifestyle news, the hot trend is "metrosexuals"—young males who are not gay but are seriously into grooming and dressing well. There are only eight documented cases of males

like this, all living in two Manhattan blocks, but they are featured in an estimated seventeen thousand newspaper and magazine articles over the course of about a week, after which this trend, like a minor character vaporized by aliens in a *Star Trek* episode, disappears and is never heard from again.

In sports, Pete Rose publishes a book in which he at last confesses to an allegation that dogged him throughout his baseball career: He's a jerk.

Speaking of shocking revelations, in . . .

FEBRUARY

. . . the nation—already troubled by bad news from Iraq, coupled with a resurgence in terrorism and a slow economic recovery—is traumatized by something that leaves a deep and lasting scar on the fragile national psyche: Janet Jackson's right nipple, which is revealed for a full three ten-thousandths of a second during the Super Bowl halftime show. This event is so traumatic that the two teams are unable to complete the game, with many players simply lying on the field in the fetal position whimpering. It is a moment reminiscent of the JFK assassination, in that virtually all Americans can remember exactly where they were when it happened.

"I was on the sofa," they say. Or: "I was in the bathroom and missed the traumatic moment, but fortunately we have TiVo."

As the nation reels in shock, the networks ban all programs that feature any kind of nudity, including unclothed fish. Congress also swiftly swings into action: Democrats blame the Bush administration, noting that the nipple was revealed on Bush's watch, while Republicans point out that during all eight years of the Clinton administration Janet Jackson clearly possessed nipples and Bill Clinton was almost certainly aware of this.

Bush himself suggests the possibility that the nipples could have originated in Iraq. John Kerry notes that there were nipples in Vietnam.

Elsewhere in politics, feisty Internet genius Howard Dean drops out of the Democratic race after losing seventeen consecutive primaries, despite leading in every single exit poll. Meanwhile, Ralph Nader announces that he will again run for president, a decision that is hailed unanimously by Nader's support base, which consists of Ralph and his friend Wendell the Talking Space Turtle.

In entertainment news, the feel-good hit of the winter is Mel Gibson's wacky film romp *The Passion of the Christ,* although critics of product placement object to the scene where Pontius Pilate can be seen holding a Diet Sprite.

On the cultural front, the mayor of San Francisco attempts to legalize same-sex marriage, which outrages those who believe that marriage is a sacred institution that should be entered into only by heterosexual people, such as Britney Spears and Mike Tyson.

Speaking of fighters, in . . .

MARCH

. . . John Kerry sews up the Democratic nomination with primary victories in California, Florida, Illinois, Canada, France, Germany, and Sweden. Kerry's closest rival, John Edwards, drops out of the race, but Dennis Kucinich stays in, saying that he intends to keep his idealistic grassroots campaign going until either all U.S. troops leave Iraq or he finds a girlfriend.

In other political news, Russian president Vladimir Putin easily wins reelection, despite exit polls indicating the winner was Howard Dean.

There is finally some positive news from Iraq, where negotiators reach agreement on an interim constitution, which guarantees that, for the first time ever, Iraq will be governed by a duly elected council of nervous men in armored cars going 80 mph.

In domestic news, U.S. gasoline prices reach record levels when, in what economists describe as a freak coincidence, two drivers attempt to refuel their Humvees on the same day.

On the legal front, a federal jury convicts Martha Stewart on four counts of needing to be taken down a peg. In what many legal experts call an unduly harsh punishment, a federal judge sentences Stewart to be the topic of two months of Jay Leno jokes.

Speaking of punishments, in . . .

APRIL

. . . the Federal Communications Commission levies a $495,000 fine against Clear Channel Communications for a 2003 incident in which Howard Stern, on his nationally broadcast radio show, exposed his right nipple.

But the big entertainment news comes at the end of the two-hour season finale of the mega-hit reality show *The Apprentice,* when Donald Trump, in the most anticipated event of the year—and quite possibly all of human history—fires that one guy, whatshisname, and keeps that other guy. You remember. It was HUGE.

Meanwhile, in another blow to the U.S.-led coalition effort in Iraq, Spain withdraws its troop, Sgt. Juan Hernandez. As violence in Iraq escalates, critics of the Bush administration charge that there are not enough U.S. soldiers over there. Administration officials heatedly deny this, arguing that the real problem is that there are too many Iraqis over there. In the words of one high-level official (who is not identified in press reports because of the difficulties involved in spelling "Condoleezza"), the administration "may have to relocate the Iraqis to a safer area, such as Ecuador." John Kerry calls this "a ridiculous idea," adding, "I wholeheartedly endorse it."

In economic news, the price of a gallon of gasoline at the pump reaches $236.97, prompting widespread concern that there is something wrong with this particular pump. Congress vows to hold hearings.

Speaking of things gone wrong, in . . .

MAY

. . . world outrage grows in reaction to photos taken inside Iraq's notorious Abu Ghraib prison showing U.S. soldiers repeatedly forcing prisoners to look at the video of Janet Jackson's right nipple. As human rights organizations voice outrage, President Bush vows to "punish whoever is responsible for this, no matter who it is, unless, of course, it is Donald Rumsfeld." Congress vows to hold hearings.

The nation's mood does not improve when the Department of Making Everybody in the Homeland Nervous raises the Official National Terror Index Level to "Yikes!" based on having received credible information indicating that al-Qaeda terrorist cells are, quote, "up to something" and "could be in your attic right now."

John Kerry, looking to improve his image with Red State voters, shoots a duck.

On the health front, medical researchers announce that if you feed one aspirin per day to laboratory rats, eventually you are going to get bit.

In sports, popular spunky horse Smarty Jones wins the

Kentucky Derby, confounding exit pollsters who had unanimously picked Seabiscuit. Congress vows to call its bookie.

The big entertainment news in May is the much-anticipated final episode of *Friends,* in which Joey, Chandler, Ross, Rachel, Monica, and Phoebe suddenly realize that they are, like, fifty-three years old.

Speaking of final episodes, in . . .

JUNE

. . . former president Ronald Reagan dies and embarks on a weeklong national tour. Also hitting the road for the last time is Ray Charles.

Another former president, Bill Clinton, travels around the nation bringing comfort to large crowds of Americans who injured themselves attempting to lift Clinton's thousand-page memoir, titled *Someday I Might Read This Myself.*

The news from Iraq continues to worsen as the interim governing council, in a move that alarms the Bush administration, chooses, by unanimous vote, its new acting president: Al Gore. He immediately demands a recount.

In a related development, CIA director George Tenet—the man who advised President Bush that the case for proving there were weapons of mass destruction in Iraq was a "slam dunk"—resigns to accept a job advising the New York Yankees.

President Bush meets with the pope and, in impromptu re-marks afterward, describes him as "a great American." John Kerry, campaigning in Michigan, strangles a deer.

On the economic front, there is good news and bad news. The good news is, the U.S. economy has generated 250,000 new jobs. The bad news is that 80 percent of these openings are for cable TV legal experts needed to speculate endlessly about Scott Peterson.

Speaking of jobseekers, in . . .

JULY

. . . John Kerry is formally nominated at the Democratic Convention in Boston and, in his acceptance speech, tells the wildly cheering delegates that, if he is elected president, his highest priority will be "to develop facial expressions." Also well received at the convention is Kerry's wife, Teresa Heinz-Ketchup Kerry, who gives a moving account of being an immigrant in America with little more than hopes, dreams, a personal staff, a large fortune, and a Gulfstream jet. Vice presidential nominee John Edwards also makes a well-received speech, after which he is never heard from again.

In Washington, President Bush, reacting to news of a projected sharp increase in the federal budget deficit, vows to find out if this is a good thing or a bad thing, or what.

On the terrorism front, the federal commission charged with investigating the Sept. 11 attacks, having spent more than a year questioning hundreds of witnesses and reviewing thousands of pages of classified documents, concludes that the attacks were "very bad" and "better not happen again." Congress vows to hold hearings.

Meanwhile, in another blow to the U.S.-led effort in Iraq, Uruguay announces that it intends to pull its troops out of the coalition. Informed that it has no troops in the coalition, Uruguay asks if it can borrow some.

In Baghdad, former Iraqi dictator Saddam Hussein appears in a courtroom to hear the charges against him, which include torture, murder, genocide, and more than 175,000 zoning violations. Hussein declares that he is innocent and offers to take a urine test. The judge rules that further proceedings will be postponed "until the Scott Peterson trial is over."

The big movie hit of the summer is *Fahrenheit 9/11,* a shocking documentary that shows how Bush administration policies were directly responsible for making Michael Moore more than $100 million.

In sports, Lance Armstrong wins his sixth consecutive Tour de France, overcoming the hardship of having to pedal hundreds of kilometers with hostile French persons clinging to his legs.

Speaking of sporting triumphs, in . . .

AUGUST

. . . Greece hosts a highly successful Olympics, with the USA winning all the gold medals, at least the ones shown on TV. Fears of terrorist attacks prove unjustified, most likely because the terrorists, like everybody else, are watching women's beach volleyball. The only major controversy involves the men's gymnastics gold medal, which is won by American Paul Hamm, despite exit polls showing it should have gone to a South Korean.

On the political front, the Republicans gather for their national convention in New York City, which welcomes them with open armpits. But the hot political story is the allegation by a group of Swift Boat veterans that John Kerry exaggerated his Vietnam accomplishments, and that, in fact, his boat was, quote, "not particularly swift." This story produces a

media frenzy of charges and countercharges that soon has the entire nation riveted to reruns of *America's Funniest Home Videos.*

In other political news, New Jersey governor James E. McGreevey resigns after confirming persistent rumors that he has nipples.

In weather news, an unprecedented series of hurricanes—Arnie, Barb, Chuck, Deb, Ernie, Francine, Gus, and Harlotta—all head directly for Florida, causing millions of Sunshine State residents, by long-standing tradition, to throng to home-supply stores in an effort to purchase the two available pieces of plywood. Damage is extensive, although experts say it would have been much worse if not for a dense protective barrier of TV news people standing on the beaches and excitedly informing the viewing audience that the wind was blowing.

In other bad news, the Department of Homeland Fear, acting on credible information, raises the National Terror Index Level to "EEEEEEEE," which is a level so high that only dogs can detect it.

Speaking of alarming, in . . .

SEPTEMBER

. . . Florida's weather woes worsen as the Sunshine State is battered on consecutive days by hurricanes Irving, Jonetta, Karl, Louanne, Myron, Naomi, Orville, Peg, and Quentin. When it is finally all over, many Florida residents are completely hairless, and shards of Disney World are coming down as far away as Montana. The federal government, reacting quickly, sends a third sheet of plywood to Florida and promises that a fourth will be on the way "soon."

In politics, the month begins with the Republican Convention and Mass Arrest still going on in New York City. The GOP delegates, confounding exit pollsters, nominate George W. Bush, who promises that, if reelected, he will "continue doing whatever it says here on the TelePrompTer."

With more bad news coming from Iraq, and Americans citing terrorism and health care as their major concerns, the news media continue their laser-beam focus on the early 1970s. Dan Rather leads the charge with a report on CBS's *60 Minutes* citing a memo, allegedly written in 1972, suggesting that Bush shirked his National Guard duty. Critics charge that the memo is a fake, pointing out that at one point it specifically mentions the 2003 OutKast hit "Hey Ya!" Rather refuses to back down, arguing that the reference could be to "an early version of the song."

Just when the public is about to abandon hope in the presidential election, the candidates get together for an actual debate at the University of Miami Convocation Center, which is the only building left standing in Florida. In summary: Bush states that being president is really, really hard, for him, anyway. Kerry states that he is really, really smart and has, like, 185 specific plans. It is agreed there will be two more debates, although nobody can explain why.

In aviation news, US Airways files for bankruptcy for a second time only to have a federal judge rule that the airline can't possibly get any more bankrupt than it already is. Meanwhile, the Transportation Security Administration, acting on credible information, announces that it will be requiring additional airport screening for commercial airline passengers who are, quote, "wearing clothes."

On the legal front, a judge drops rape charges against Kobe Bryant on the grounds that "the Scott Peterson trial is hogging all the cable-TV celebrity legal analysts."

In medical news, the popular antiarthritis drug Vioxx is pulled from the market after clinical trials show that it may contain carbohydrates. On a more positive note, former president Bill Clinton experiences chest pains and is rushed to New York–Presbyterian Hospital, where, in a five-hour operation, surgeons successfully remove a glazed doughnut the size of a catcher's mitt.

Speaking of the National Pastime, in . . .

OCTOBER

. . . the Boston Red Sox, ending an eighty-six-year drought, defeat the St. Louis Cardinals to win the World Series, defying exit polls that had overwhelmingly picked the Green Bay Packers. The Red Sox get into the Series thanks to the fact that the New York Yankees—who were leading the American League championships three games to none, and have all-stars at every position, not to mention a payroll larger than the gross national product of Sweden—chose that particular time to execute the most spectacular choke in all of sports history, an unbelievable Gag-o-Rama, a noxious nosedive, a pathetic gut-check failure of such epic dimensions that every thinking human outside of the New York metropolitan area experienced a near-orgasmic level of happiness. But there is no need to rub it in.

In entertainment news, Howard Stern signs a five-year, $500 million deal to move his show to satellite radio, where a man can still display a nipple.

On the health front, the big story is a nationwide shortage of flu vaccine, caused by the fact that apparently all the flu vaccine in the world is manufactured by some guy in Wales or someplace with a Bunsen burner. Congress, acting with unusual swiftness, calls on young, healthy Americans to forego getting flu shots this year so that more vaccine will be available for members of Congress.

President Bush notes that additional vaccine "could be hidden somewhere in Iraq."

John Kerry, campaigning in North Carolina, kills a raccoon with a hatchet.

In aviation news, *SpaceShipOne,* the first privately funded manned rocket, breaks free from its mother plane, soars sixty-two miles above the Earth, swoops gracefully back to Earth, rolls to a stop on the Mojave Desert, and files for bankruptcy.

Abroad, Yasser Arafat collapses and is taken to a hospital, where his condition rapidly worsens, and continues to worsen until nobody thinks it can get any worse, but somehow it does. "It's really bad," says a hospital spokesperson. "We've never seen anybody achieve this degree of worsening without kicking the actual bucket."

Osama bin Laden, who has not been seen or heard from in quite a while, releases a video in which he states that he is "willing to listen to offers from satellite radio."

In other international news, Afghanistan's historic first democratic elections go off without a hitch, except for an unexplained 27,500 votes from residents of Palm Beach County.

Speaking of elections, in . . .

NOVEMBER

. . . the 2004 U.S. presidential election campaign, which has been going on since the early stages of the Cher Farewell Tour, finally staggers to the finish line. John Kerry easily sweeps to a fifty-three-state landslide victory in the exit polls and has pretty much picked out his new cabinet when word begins to leak out that the actual, physical voters have elected George W. Bush. Democrats struggle to understand how this could have happened, and, after undergoing a harsh and unsparing self-examination, conclude that Red State residents are morons. Some Democrats threaten to move to Canada; Republicans, in a gracious gesture of reconciliation, offer to help them pack.

The postelection recriminations and name-calling continue for more than a week until finally the public, realizing that there are still important issues that affect the entire nation, returns its attention to the Scott Peterson trial, which finally ends with the jury finding Peterson guilty of being just unbelievably irritating. The verdict means sudden unemployment for thousands of cable news legal analysts, who return to their cave to hang upside down by day and suck cow blood by night until they are called for the next big TV trial.

Meanwhile, there are big changes in the Bush cabinet, the most notable involving Secretary of State Colin Powell, who announces his resignation after returning from a trip to find all his office furniture replaced by Condoleezza Rice's. Attorney General John Ashcroft also announces that he will leave the cabinet to resume private life as a frozen haddock.

Dan Rather also resigns, on orders received via the secret radio in his teeth.

In other presidential news, thousands attend a festive ded-

ication of the seventy-thousand-square-foot William Jefferson Clinton Presidential Library in Little Rock, Ark., next door to the ninety-thousand-square-foot William Jefferson Clinton Presidential Cafeteria.

As the nation enters the holiday season, the festive mood is dampened by the intrusion of grim reality, as 137 Americans die in vicious predawn aisle-to-aisle combat over deeply discounted post-Thanksgiving Christmas sale items. Congress vows to remain on recess.

Abroad, the big news is the presidential election in the Ukraine, where the government, citing exit polls, declares that Viktor Yanukovych has defeated Viktor Yushchenko. Hundreds of thousands of outraged Ukrainians take to the streets, protesting the fact that they cannot remember which Viktor is which. Many threaten to move to Canada.

Meanwhile, the condition of Yasser Arafat, already worse than anybody believed possible, somehow worsens still more, until it becomes so bad that Arafat no longer responds to a medical procedure known technically as the Hatpin Test, at which point he is declared legally deceased. After a funeral service attended by a large and extremely enthusiastic crowd, he is buried in several locations.

In sports, a Pacers–Pistons NBA game in Detroit turns into a riot after Pacers star and rocket scientist Ron Artest, hit by a cup thrown by Fan A, retaliates by charging into the stands and attacking Fans B, C, and D. Explaining his actions later on

The Today Show, Artest says he thought he "saw weapons of mass destruction."

Speaking of sportsmanship, in . . .

DECEMBER

. . . the pro-baseball world is stunned by the unbelievably shocking and astounding and totally unexpected news that some players may have taken steroids. "Gosh," exclaims baseball commissioner Bud "Bud" Selig, "this could explain why so many players suddenly develop two hundred additional pounds of pure muscle and, in some cases, a tail." Seeking to restore fan confidence in the sport, the players' union and the team owners, in a rare display of cooperation, agree that it will be necessary to raise ticket prices.

In Washington, the cabinet shuffle continues as John Hargrove resigns as secretary of interstate affairs upon being informed, after four years in Washington, that there is no such cabinet position. "Under the circumstances," states President Bush, "he did a heckuva job."

On the military front, the president, in a move that sparks international outrage, announces that he is sending Ron Artest to Iraq. Meanwhile, the dollar continues to decline abroad, largely because of what U.S. Treasury secretary John Snow describes as "French waiters."

In other international news, Iran continues to heatedly

deny that it is developing nuclear weapons but is unable to offer a plausible explanation as to why it purchased two hundred pounds of enriched uranium on eBay. The United Nations, reacting to this crisis with unusual swiftness, resolves to do nothing.

In the Ukraine, weeks of massive street protests finally lead to a ruling by the Ukrainian supreme court that there must be a new election between the two Viktors, only this time "they have to wear name tags." The protesters attempt to go back indoors only to discover that their shoes are frozen to the streets.

Meanwhile, Yasser Arafat continues to worsen.

And he is not alone. As we look back on the events of 2004, we sometimes get the feeling that the whole world is worsening. It would be easy to become depressed about the future, and yet . . .

. . . and yet we are not. As we approach the end of the year, we find ourselves feeling hope, optimism, and a warm glow of happiness. Why? Because we've been hitting the eggnog. We recommend you do the same. But whatever you do: Have a Happy New Year.

2005

WILMA, RITA, KATRINA: NO MATTER HOW YOU STACK IT UP, 2005 BLEW

I t was the Year of the Woman. But not in a good way.

Oh, I'm not saying that men did nothing stupid or despicable in 2005. Of course they did! That's why we call them "men."

But women are supposed to be *better* than men. Women are the backbone of civilization: They keep families together, nurture relationships, uphold basic standards of morality, and go to the bathroom without making noise. Women traditionally shun the kinds of pointless, brutal, destructive activities that so often involve men, such as mass murder and fantasy football.

But not this year. Women got CRAZY this year. Consider

some of the more disturbing stories from 2005 and look at the names connected with them: Martha Stewart. Judith Miller. Valerie Plame. Jennifer "Runaway Bride" Wilbanks. Paris Hilton. Greta "All Natalee Holloway All the Time" Van Susteren. Harriet Miers. Katrina. Rita. Wilma. Michael Jackson.

Of course, not all the alarming stories from 2005 involved women. Some of them involved men, and at least one of those men was named "Scooter." I'll be honest: I don't really know who "Scooter" is or what he allegedly did. He's involved in one of those Washington, D.C.–style scandals that are very, very important, but way too complicated for regular non-

Beltway humans to comprehend. You try to read a Scooter story and next thing you know you're emerging from a coma weeks later with spiders nesting in your ears. But whatever Scooter allegedly did, it was bad. We know this because pretty much all the news this year was bad. Oh, sure, there were some positive developments. Here is a complete list:

- In some areas, the price of gasoline, much of the time, remained below $5 a gallon.
- Nobody you know caught avian flu. Yet.
- The Yankees once again failed to win the World Series.
- Cher actually ended her farewell tour.

That was it for the good news. The rest of 2005 was a steady diet of misery, horror, and despair, leavened occasionally by deep anxiety. So, just for fun, let's take a look back, starting with . . .

JANUARY

. . . when President George W. Bush is sworn in for a second term, pledging in his inauguration speech that, over the next four years, he will continue, to the best of his ability, trying to pronounce big words. In a strongly worded rebuttal, the Democratic leadership points out that when you get right down to it, there IS no Democratic leadership.

In other government news, President Bush's nominee to be U.S. attorney general, Alberto Gonzales, undergoes a grueling Senate hearing in which Democrats probe him repeatedly about his views on torture. At one point, the Democrats threaten that if Gonzales does not give them the information they want, they will force him to listen, without ear protection, to a question from Sen. Joe Biden. "No!" screams Gonzales. "Anything but that!"

On the social front, Donald Trump, in a lavish ceremony attended by many celebrities and helicopter pilots, marries his third or fourth wife, the lovely Mrs. Trophy Supermodel Trump. After the traditional Blessing of the Prenup, the couple retires to the honeymoon suite for an intimate evening involving champagne, scented candles, and a team of eight apprentices.

Johnny Carson, an oasis of wit in the wasteland, signs off for good.

In sports, the winner of the Orange Bowl—and thus the national college football championship—is Lance Armstrong, who is once again suspected of being on something.

Meanwhile, in Iraq, the first free elections in half a century are held under tense but generally scary conditions, with more than eight million Iraqis turning out to elect a National Assembly, whose idealistic goal in the coming months will be to not get blown up.

But the mood is more upbeat in . . .

FEBRUARY

. . . which dawns on a hopeful note in the Middle East, where Israelis and Palestinians, after decades of bitter violence and short-lived truces, are finally able to . . .

Never mind.

In other hopeful news, President Bush, seeking to patch up the troubled relationship between the United States and its European allies, embarks on a four-nation tour. When critics note that two of the nations are not actually located in Europe, the White House responds that the president was "acting on the best intelligence available at the time."

On the domestic front, the president proposes, in his State of the Union speech, a plan to privatize Social Security so that it will be, quote, "more privatized." In response, the Democratic leadership pledges to churn out irate press releases for a while, then totally loses interest. Within hours, Washington is back to normal as both sides resume the tedious but important bipartisan work of jacking up the federal deficit.

In sports, the Super Bowl is held for the first time in Jacksonville. Defying critics who mocked it as a backwater hick town, Jacksonville manages to host a fine event, marred only by the 143 spectators killed or wounded during the halftime raccoon shoot.

On the social front, Prince Charles gets formally engaged

to Camilla Parker Bowles. The British public responds with sincere and heartfelt wishes that the happy couple will not reproduce.

In New York's Central Park, the artists Christo and Jeanne-Claude create *The Gates*—a twenty-three-mile-long work consisting of 7,503 fabric-draped metal structures. Within twenty minutes, every single one of these structures has been urinated on by a dog.

A study by researchers at the University of Utah proves what many people have long suspected: Everybody talking on a cell phone, except you, is a moron.

Meanwhile, as the nationwide identity theft epidemic worsens, FBI director Robert S. Mueller III pledges that he will make it the top priority of the bureau to find, and prosecute, the individuals charging stuff to his American Express card.

Speaking of financial hanky-panky, in . . .

MARCH

. . . a federal jury convicts former WorldCom executive Bernie Ebbers in connection with an $11 billion fraud that led to the bankruptcy of the telecom giant. Upon Ebbers's arrival at the federal prison, nearly $7 billion is recovered during what shaken guards later describe as "the cavity search from hell."

In economic news, financially troubled Delta Airlines announces that it will no longer offer pillows on its flights because passengers keep eating them. But the economy gets a boost when the jobless rate plummets, as hundreds of thousands of unemployed cable TV legal experts are hired to comment on the trial of Michael Jackson. Jackson is charged with ten counts of being a space alien freakadelic weirdo. Everybody agrees this will be very difficult to prove in California.

In a related story, a California jury finds that actor Robert Blake did not kill his wife. The jury also rules that John Wilkes Booth had nothing to do with the Lincoln assassination and that bears do not poop in the woods. In other celebrity legal news, Martha Stewart is released from prison. The next morning, in a chilling coincidence, all of the witnesses who testified against Martha wake up and discover, to their utter horror, that their sheets no longer match their pillowcases.

Meanwhile, in Washington, the U.S. House of Representatives takes time out from jacking up the deficit to look into the baffling mystery of whether professional baseball players suddenly develop gigantic muscles because they use steroids, or what. Former St. Louis Cardinal star Mark McGwire, who once held the major-league record for most home runs in a single season, arouses suspicions when he repeatedly denies, under oath, that he ever played professional baseball.

But the major issue facing our elected leaders in March clearly is not whether a bunch of overpaid athletes cheated. No, at a time when the nation is beset by serious problems in

so many critical areas—including Iraq, terrorism, the economy, energy, education, and health care—the issue that obsesses our elected leaders to the point of paralyzing government at the federal, state, and local levels for weeks is: Terri Schiavo's feeding tube. This, unfortunately, is not a joke.

In entertainment news, controversial anchorman Dan Rather retires from CBS News with a poignant farewell speech, cut short when he is teleported up to the Mothership.

Speaking of people who read from TelePrompTers, in . . .

APRIL

... President Bush, in a decisive response to sharply rising gasoline prices, delivers a major speech proposing that Americans switch to nuclear-powered cars. In a strongly worded rebuttal, angry congressional Democrats state that because of a scheduling mix-up, they missed the president's speech, but whatever he said they totally disagree with it, and if they once voted in favor of it they did so only because the president lied to them.

In other Washington news, the U.S. Senate approves the appointment of John Negroponte to become the nation's first intelligence czar. His immediate task is to locate his office, which, according to a dossier compiled by the CIA, FBI, NSA, and military intelligence, is, quote, "probably somewhere in the United States or Belgium."

On the economic front, financially troubled Delta Air Lines switches to pay toilets on domestic flights.

In Rome, the College of Cardinals gathers following the death of beloved pope John Paul II. As the world waits breathlessly, the cardinals, after two days of secret deliberations, order white smoke to be sent up the Sistine Chapel chimney, signaling that they have made their decision: Robert Blake is definitely guilty.

In sports, Tiger Woods claims his fourth Masters title with

a dramatic play-off win over a surprisingly dogged Lance Armstrong.

As April draws to a close, the nation focuses its eyeballs on bride-to-be Jennifer Wilbanks, whose claim that she was abducted just before her wedding is undermined by a widely circulated photo of her in which her pupils appear to be the size of dinner plates. When it becomes clear that nothing actually happened—that there was no abduction and that Wilbanks is basically just a troubled person—the news media drop the story and move on to more important matters.

Ha-ha! Seriously, as April morphs into . . .

MAY

. . . the Runaway Bride story totally dominates the news, becoming so gigantically huge that some cable TV news shows are forced to divert precious resources from the Michael Jackson trial. But in the end sanity prevails, and Wilbanks is forced to accept responsibility for the trouble she has caused, ultimately selling media rights to her story for a reported $500,000.

In other show business news, millions of middle-aged people without dates wet their Luke Skywalker–model underpants with joy as they view the final installment of the beloved *Star Wars* series, *Star Wars MXCVII: Enough Already.* Fans hail it as the least tedious *Star Wars* in decades; many are stunned by the surprise ending, when it turns out that Darth Vader is actually Robert Blake. Director George Lucas announces that, having fulfilled his artistic dream, he will now retire and learn to write dialogue.

Tom Cruise, seeking to counter the increasingly widespread view that he is an orbiting space module, jumps up and down on Oprah's couch.

In world news, members of the newly elected Iraqi parliament demonstrate a surprisingly sophisticated grasp of the principles of American-style democracy by voting to build a $223 million bridge to a virtually uninhabited island off the coast of Alaska.

Elsewhere abroad, European Union leaders are stunned when the proposed EU constitution is overwhelmingly rejected by French voters, who apparently do not care for the Deodorant Clause. President Bush visits Russia for an important photo opportunity, after which he describes Russia as "a foreign country where they speak Russian," an assertion that is immediately challenged by congressional Democrats.

The U.S. Senate reaches an agreement ending a stalemate over the confirmation of Bush-appointed judges, thus avoiding the so-called nuclear option, according to which Sen. Joe Biden would be allowed to ask a question, thereby shutting the federal government down for months.

Financially troubled Delta Air Lines, hoping to boost ticket sales, introduces a new "student discount" fare, which will apply to flights where the airplane is being flown by student pilots.

In media news, the editor of *Newsweek* magazine retracts a report that guards at the Guantánamo Bay prison flushed a Koran down a toilet in front of a Muslim detainee. "It turns out," the editor states, "that it was actually the *detainee* who was flushed down the toilet. Boy, is our face red!"

But the biggest media shocker occurs when "Deep Throat," the Watergate source whose identity has been a tantalizing secret for more than thirty years, is finally revealed—in a stunning and unforgettable development that sends shock waves of shock throughout the world—to be . . . Let me just check Google here . . . OK, it was some guy nobody ever heard of. But it was *totally* unexpected.

Speaking of unexpected, in . . .

JUNE

. . . a California jury acquits Michael Jackson on all charges of everything, including any crimes he may or may not commit in the future. "We simply felt that the prosecution did not prove its case," states the jury foreman, Robert Blake. Jackson announces that he no longer feels welcome in the United States and will move to another dimension.

In disturbing medical news, a new study of one thousand

Americans finds that obesity in the United States has gotten so bad that there actually were, upon closer scrutiny, only six hundred Americans involved in the study.

On the economic front, financially troubled Delta Air Lines, looking to reduce skyrocketing fuel costs, introduces a new "no frills" glider service, offering daily flights from Atlanta to "some location between one and fifteen miles from Atlanta."

Meanwhile, the U.S. film industry, in the midst of the worst box office slump in twenty years, looks for possible explanations as to why Americans are not flocking to movie theaters. In a totally unrelated development, *The Adventures of Sharkboy and Lavagirl* opens nationwide, to be followed in coming months by *The Dukes of Hazzard* and *Deuce Bigalow: European Gigolo*.

Israeli and Palestinian leaders reach an agreement under which Israel will withdraw its settlers from the Gaza Strip, arousing peace hopes in amnesia victims everywhere. In response to this historic development, Fox newsperson Greta Van Susteren heads for Aruba to report personally on the Natalee Holloway disappearance.

Hurricane season officially begins, with a spokesman for the National Hurricane Center warning that, quote, "This could be one of the most active sEEEEEEEEE . . ." His body is never found.

The U.S. Supreme Court, in a Solomonic ruling on a display of the Ten Commandments at the Texas Capitol, allows the display to remain, but orders the state to correct all 137 spelling errors. The Supreme Court remains in the news in . . .

JULY

. . . when Justice Sandra Day O'Connor announces her retirement, setting off a heated debate between right-wing groups who think the president should appoint a conservative to replace her and left-wing groups who think the president should drop dead. Eventually, Bush nominates a man going by the moniker of "John Roberts," who, in the tradition of recent Supreme Court nominees, refuses to reveal anything about himself and wears a Zorro-style mask to protect his secret identity. In response, Democrats on the Senate Judiciary Committee, led by Sen. Joe Biden, vow to, quote, "get on television A LOT."

But the juiciest story by far in Washington is the riveting scandal involving *New York Times* reporter Judith Miller, who is jailed for refusing to answer questions before a grand jury, called by special prosecutor Patrick Fitzgerald, who is trying to find out whether the name of CIA agent Valerie Plame was leaked to columnist Robert Novak by an administration source such as presidential confidants Karl Rove or Ari Fleischer, or Lewis "Scooter" Libby, chief of staff to vice president Dick "Dick" Cheney, in an effort to discredit Plame's husband, former ambassador Joseph Wilson, in connection with the use of allegedly unreliable documents concerning ... Hey! Wake up! This is important!

Anyway, this scandal totally rivets everybody in Washington, D.C., although it fails to gain traction in the continental United States, where the average citizen has enough trouble remembering his e-mail password and is not about to waste precious brain cells on Scooter.

The troubled U.S. manned-spaceflight program hits yet another snag when, moments before the "return to space" launch of space shuttle *Discovery*, a technician notices that the shuttle and its booster rockets are pointed at the ground, instead of space. The launch is delayed for several days while workers repaint the THIS SIDE UP arrows.

In weather news, the formation of Hurricane Dennis is followed closely by the formation of Hurricane Emily, arousing suspicions among some staffers at headquarters of the Federal Emergency Management Agency (FEMA) that hurricane season might be going on. It is agreed that somebody probably should look into this and write a report no later than Halloween.

Abroad, the news from London is grim as four terrorist bombs wreak deadly havoc on the city's transit systems, prompting Greta Van Susteren to do a series of urgent personal reports from Aruba on how these attacks could affect the investigation into the Natalee Holloway disappearance.

In sports, Lance Armstrong rides down the Champs-Elysées, raising his arms in a triumphant gesture, which causes the French army to surrender instantly.

No, sorry; that was a cheap shot. One unit held out for nearly an hour.

In book news, millions of youngsters snap up the latest in the Harry Potter series, *Harry Potter Must Be, Like, 32 Years Old by Now*. The book has a surprise plot twist that upsets some fans: Beloved Hogwarts headmaster Albus Dumbledore is killed by Severus Snape, who, moments later, is acquitted by a California jury.

Speaking of surprises that nobody could have predicted, in . . .

AUGUST

. . . Baltimore Orioles star Rafael Palmeiro, who vigorously denied steroid use when he testified before Congress in March, is forced to change his story when, in the seventh inning of a game against Cleveland, both of his forearms explode.

Meanwhile, in yet another blow to the troubled U.S. manned-spaceflight program, a *Discovery* crew member is forced to undertake a risky space walk when a technician notices a terrified NASA painter clinging to the shuttle fuselage. Then, because of bad weather, *Discovery* must divert from Cape

Canaveral and land at Chicago's O'Hare Airport, where the crew is forced to wait for nearly two hours at baggage claim. NASA suspends the shuttle program, saying it will look into other options, including a possible joint venture with Delta Air Lines.

In other science news, South Korean scientists—I am not making this item up—clone a dog. This one is too easy.

In Washington, President Bush bypasses Congress with a recess appointment of his controversial nominee John Bolton to be U.S. ambassador to the United Nations. Bolton immediately signals a new tone in American diplomacy by punching

out the ambassador from Yemen in a dispute involving the UN cafeteria salad bar.

In other foreign-policy news, the Rev. Pat Robertson states on his Christian Broadcasting Network show that the U.S. should assassinate Venezuelan president Hugo Chávez. Responding to harsh criticism, the Rev. Robertson retracts this statement several days later with the explanation, "Evidently, I am a raving lunatic."

On the economic front, there is bad news and good news. The bad news is, gasoline prices are reaching $3 a gallon. The good news is, with the manufacturer's rebate, you can buy a new Hummer for $167.

But by far the biggest story in August is Hurricane Katrina, a massive, deadly storm that thrashes Florida, then heads into the Gulf of Mexico. For decades, experts have been warning that such a storm, if it were to hit New Orleans, would devastate the city; now it becomes clear that this is exactly what is about to happen. For days, meteorologists are on television warning, dozens of times per hour, that Katrina will, in fact, hit New Orleans with devastating results. Armed with this advance knowledge, government officials at the local, state, and federal levels are in a position to be totally, utterly shocked when Katrina—of all things—devastates New Orleans. For several days, chaos reigns, with most of the relief effort taking the form of Geraldo Rivera, who, by his own estimate, saves more than 170,000 people.

FEMA director Michael Brown, after conducting an aerial

survey, reports that "the situation is improving," only to be informed that the area he surveyed was actually Phoenix. For her part, Greta Van Susteren personally broadcasts many timely reports from Aruba on how the Katrina devastation will affect the ongoing Natalee Holloway investigation.

It is not until . . .

SEPTEMBER

. . . that the full magnitude of the New Orleans devastation sinks in and local, state, and federal officials manage to get their act together and begin the difficult, painstaking work of blaming each other for screwing up. Urged on by President Bush, Congress votes to spend what could wind up being more than $200 billion to repair the Gulf Coast and fix up New Orleans so that it will be just as good as new when the next devastating hurricane devastates it.

With the horror of Katrina fresh in everyone's mind, a new hurricane, Rita, draws a bead on the Gulf Coast, causing millions of panicky Texans to get into their cars and flee an average distance of 150 feet before they become stuck in a monster traffic jam, where some remain for more than twelve hours. "It was hell," reports one traumatized victim. "The classic rock station played 'Daydream Believer,' like, fifty-three freaking times."

President Bush, after an aerial tour of the devastated region, tells reporters that he always kind of liked "Daydream Believer."

In nonhurricane news, the Senate confirms the Supreme Court nominee known as "John Roberts" after the Judiciary Committee spends several fruitless days trying to trick him into expressing an opinion by asking trap questions such as "Can you tell us the capital of Vermont and your views on abortion?" The only moment of drama comes when Sen. Joe Biden launches into his opening remarks, thus causing several committee members, who forgot to insert earplugs, to lapse into comas.

In other political news, Republicans, already wounded by a series of ethical scandals, are dealt yet another blow when House majority leader Tom DeLay is indicted for robbing a convenience store. DeLay insists that this is a common practice in Congress; indignant Democrats respond that they can prove they were playing poker on the night in question. None of this is expected to seriously impact the Natalee Holloway investigation, according to Greta Van Susteren, reporting live from Aruba.

The month's biggest drama takes place at Los Angeles International Airport, where, as millions of people watch on live TV, a JetBlue airliner with the nose wheel turned sideways manages to land safely, after which it is immediately purchased by NASA.

In international news, North Korea, following months of negotiations with the U.S. and other concerned nations, agrees to stop producing nuclear weapons in exchange for one of those new iPods. The United Nations Security Council censures John Bolton for giving noogies to the ambassador from Sweden.

Speaking of appointees, in . . .

OCTOBER

. . . President Bush, needing to make another appointment to the Supreme Court, conducts a thorough and painstaking investigation of every single woman lawyer within an eight-foot radius of his desk. He concludes that the best person for the job is White House counsel Harriet Miers, who, in the tradition of such legendary justices as Felix Frankfurter, Louis Brandeis, and Oliver Wendell Holmes, is a carbon-based life-form.

The nomination immediately runs into trouble when Miers, though reportedly a nice churchgoing person and a good bowler, turns out to be not such an expert on constitutional law, at one point expressing the view that the Fourth Amendment requires restaurant employees to wash their hands after using the restroom. (In fact, it is the Seventh Amendment.)

Ultimately, Miers withdraws her name. The president, after conducting another exhaustive search, decides to appoint "John Roberts" again, because it worked out so well the first time. Informed by his aides that there could be some legal problem with this tactic, the president finally decides to nominate Samuel Alito. Democrats immediately announce that they strongly oppose Alito and intend to do some research soon to find out why.

In Congress, Tom DeLay's ethical woes worsen as he is indicted on additional charges of hijacking a train.

As fears of a worldwide avian flu epidemic mount, the surgeon general warns Americans against having unprotected sex with birds. Fortunately, there is no sign yet of the deadly disease on Aruba, thus allowing the Natalee Holloway investigation to continue unimpeded, according to on-the-scene reporter Greta Van Susteren.

In Iraq, Saddam Hussein goes on trial, facing charges of genocide, human rights violations, and failure to pay more than $173 billion in parking tickets. In his opening statement, the defiant former dictator tells the court he intends to prove that these crimes were actually committed by Tom DeLay.

On the weather front, Hurricane Wilma blasts across Florida, knocking out power to the eight homes that still had electricity after the seventeen previous hurricanes to hit the state this year. Critics, noting that Wilma was not a particularly strong storm, ask why Florida Power & Light's utility poles seem to fall down every time a moth passes gas. FPL officials attempt to answer these charges in a press conference but their microphones keep tipping over.

In sports, the National Hockey League, amid much hoopla, resumes play, fueling rumors that the league must have, at some point, stopped playing. Immediately, dozens of fights break out, all of them won by Lance Armstrong.

Speaking of conflict, in . . .

NOVEMBER

. . . Americans find themselves heatedly debating a difficult question: Is it truly in the nation's best interests for its citizens to be fighting, and suffering heavy casualties, to achieve the elusive—some say impossible—goal of buying a laptop computer marked down to $300 at Wal-Mart the day after

Thanksgiving? For many Americans, the answer is a resounding yes, as they observe the official start of the Christmas shopping season at 5 a.m. on Nov. 25 with the traditional Trampling of the Elderly, Slow-Moving Shoppers while the mall p.a. system interrupts "O Come, All Ye Faithful" with urgent requests for paramedics. The season's hottest gift is the Microsoft Xbox 360 gaming system, which is in big demand because (1) it's really cool and (2) Microsoft apparently made, like, three of them.

Also heating up in November is the debate over Iraq, with even Vice President Dick Cheney joining in, fueling rumors that he is still alive. President Bush makes a series of strong speeches, stating that while he "will not impugn the patriotism" of those who oppose his administration's policies, they are "traitor scum." This outrages congressional Democrats, who respond with a two-pronged strategy of (1) demanding that the troops be brought home and (2) voting overwhelmingly against a resolution to bring the troops home.

True item: During the debate on Iraq, Rep. Marion Berry (D-Ark.) calls Rep. Jeb Hensarling (R-Tex.) "a Howdy Doody–looking nimrod."

Tom DeLay is indicted for cattle rustling.

Abroad, unemployed ghetto youths in France go on a weeks-long rampage, burning thousands of cars to express their view that being an unemployed French ghetto youth sucks. Outraged, French president Jacques Chirac announces that, as a precautionary move, he is relocating the army to

Belgium. This is expected to have little impact on the ongoing Natalee Holloway investigation, according to Greta Van Susteren's sources in Aruba.

In one of the month's more bizarre stories, a luxury cruise ship off the coast of Somalia is attacked by pirates in inflatable boats. The pirates are armed with machine guns and grenade launchers; unfortunately for them, the passengers are armed with cruise-ship food. The pirates barely escape with their lives under a deadly hail of falling entrées, including slabs of prime rib the size of queen mattresses.

Absolutely true November item: Michael "Heckuva Job" Brown, who resigned after being harshly criticized for his performance as FEMA director following Katrina, announces that he is starting a consulting business that will—you are going to think I'm making this up but I'm not—advise clients on preparing for disasters.

And "disaster" is clearly the word for . . .

DECEMBER

. . . which begins on a troubling economic note as General Motors, the world's largest automaker, announces that, despite a massive program of rebates, zero-interest financing, employee discounts, lifetime mechanical warranties, and dealer incentives, it has not actually sold a car since March of 1998. "We're in real trouble," states troubled CEO Rick Wagoner, adding: "Even I drive a Kia."

In other troubling financial news, Delta Air Lines announces a plan to convert its entire fleet of planes to condominiums. Within hours, the housing bubble bursts.

The hurricane season, which has produced so many storms that the National Weather Service is now naming them after fraternities, fails to end as scheduled as yet another hurricane, Epsilon, forms in the Atlantic. The good news is that Epsilon poses no threat whatsoever to land. The bad news is, it still manages to knock out power to most of South Florida.

In politics, Republicans and Democrats debate the war in Iraq with increasing bitterness, although both sides agree on the critical importance, with American troops in harm's way, of continuing to jack up the deficit. Tom DeLay flees to California, where a friendly jury agrees to hide him in the barn until things cool off.

Abroad, Western nations become increasingly suspicious that Iran is developing nuclear weapons when a giant mushroom cloud rises over the Iranian desert. The Iranian government quickly issues a statement explaining that the cloud was caused by, quote, "mushrooms." As a precautionary measure, France surrenders anyway.

In Iraq, the trial of ex-dictator Saddam Hussein takes a dramatic turn when surprise prosecution witness Kato Kaelin testifies that, to the best of his knowledge, Hussein was at the scene when the alleged crimes took place. Under cross-examination, however, Kaelin states that, also to the best of his knowledge, the Kurds are "the band that did 'Who Let the Dogs Out.'" An outraged Hussein orders everybody in the courtroom to be beheaded and shot, then chuckles sheepishly when he remembers that he no longer has the authority to do this.

Greta Van Susteren is elected prime minister of Aruba.

As the troubled year draws to a troubling close, yet another hurricane, Kappa Sigma Gamma, forms in the South Atlantic, threatening to blast the U.S. mainland with a load of energy that, according to the National Hurricane Center, is the equivalent of seventeen trillion six-packs of Bud Light. On an even more ominous note, officials of the World Health Organization reveal that—in what disease researchers have been calling "the nightmare scenario"—a mad cow has become infected with bird flu. "We don't want to cause panic," state the officials, "but we give the human race six weeks, tops."

So, OK, we're doomed. But look at the upside: If humanity becomes extinct, there's a chance that Paris Hilton will, too. So put on your party hat, raise your champagne glass, and join with me in this festive toast: Happy New Year!

Or however long it lasts.

2006

A BOLD NEW DIRECTION!

OR, NOT!

I t was a momentous year, a year of events that will echo in the annals of history the way a dropped plate of calamari echoes in an Italian restaurant with a tile floor. Decades from now, our grandchildren will come to us and say, "Tell us, Grandpa or Grandma as the case may be, what it was like to be alive in the year that Angelina Jolie, Tom Cruise, Brad Pitt, Britney Spears, and Katie whatshername all had babies, although not necessarily in those combinations." And we will smile wisely and emit a streamer of drool, because we will be very old and unable to hear them.

And that will be a good thing, because there are many things about 2006 that we will not want to remember. This was the year in which the members of the United States Congress, who do not bother to read the actual bills they pass, spent weeks poring over instant messages sent by a pervert. This was the year in which the vice president of the United States shot a lawyer, which turned out to be totally legal in Texas. This was the year in which there came to be essentially no difference between the treatment of maximum security prison inmates and the treatment of commercial airline passengers.

This was the year in which—as clearly foretold in the Bible as a sign of the Apocalypse—Howie Mandel got a hit TV show.

Also, there were many pesky problems left over from 2005 that refused to go away in 2006, including Iraq, immigration, high gas prices, terrorism, global warming, avian flu, Iran, North Korea, and Paris Hilton. Future generations are going to look back at this era and ask us how we could have allowed Paris Hilton to happen and we are not going to have a good answer.

Did anything good happen in 2006? Let me think. No. But before we move on to 2007, let's take a moment to reflect back on the historic events, real and imaginary, of this historic year, starting with . . .

JANUARY

. . . a month that dawns with petty partisan bickering in Washington, D.C., a place where many people view petty partisan bickering as honest, productive work, like making furniture. The immediate cause of the bickering is the Republican ethics scandal involving lobbyist Jack Abramoff and House Majority Leader Tom DeLay, both of whom you can tell, just by looking at them, are guilty of something. The Democrats charge that the Republicans have created a "Culture of Corruption" and should be thrown out of office so the Democrats can return to power and run the scandal-free style of government for which they are so famous. The Republicans respond that the Democrats are soft on terrorism soft on terrorism soft on terrorism softonterrorism. Both sides issue press releases far into the night.

The other big focus of the bickering is the nomination of Samuel Alito to the Supreme Court. As always, the Senate Judiciary Committee hearings provide high-quality TV entertainment as the nation tunes in to see if Sen. Edward M. Kennedy will be able to successfully remember the nominee's name. The bulk of the hearings are spent in the traditional manner, with Democrats trying to trick the nominee into revealing his views on abortion and Republicans reminding the nominee that he does not have to reveal his views on abortion. The subsequent exchange of press releases is so intense that several government photocopiers burst into flames.

In the War on Terror, Osama bin Laden, who may or may not be dead, nevertheless releases another audiotape, for the first time making it downloadable from iTunes. Bin Laden also starts a blog, in which he calls upon his followers to destroy the corrupt Infidels and also try to find out how a person, hypothetically, can get Chinese food delivered to a cave.

In the Middle East, Palestinian voters elect the militant Hamas Party, which assumes control of government functions such as street repair, which Hamas decides to handle by firing rockets at potholes. Canada also holds elections, which are won by some Canadian, we assume.

In economic news, the big story is the retirement of Federal Reserve Board chairman Alan Greenspan, who, after nineteen years as the person most responsible for guiding the

American economy, steps down, taking with him the thanks of a grateful nation and a suitcase containing $11 billion. But the financial news is not so good in . . .

FEBRUARY

. . . when President Bush, delivering what is billed as a "major address on energy policy," reveals that the nation has an "addiction" to "foreign oil," which comes from "foreign countries" located "outside of the United States" that are getting this oil from "under the ground." To combat this problem, the president proposes the development of "new technology" in the form of "inventions," such as "a Lincoln Navigator that gets 827 miles per gallon," although he allows that this could "take time."

But this bold energy initiative does not get nearly as much attention as the administration's decision to allow a company owned by the United Arab Emirates to operate six U.S. seaports. This outrages Congress, which briefly ceases partisan bickering to demand that the White House return control of the ports, in the interest of national security, to Anthony Soprano.

Speaking of guys who avoid the limelight: Vice President Dick Cheney, attempting to bring down a quail with a shotgun, shoots attorney Harry Whittington. Local authorities rule the shooting was an accident, noting that if the vice president was going to intentionally shoot somebody it would be Nancy Pelosi. The quail is eventually tracked down and vaporized by an F-16.

Internationally, the big news comes from Denmark, center of a mounting furor over some cartoons, published the previous year in a Danish newspaper, which depict a prophet whom, in the interest of not offending anybody, we will refer to as Fohammed. This upsets several million of the prophet's followers, who request a formal apology from the newspaper, greater sensitivity to their religious beliefs, and, where necessary, beheadings. Eventually, everybody realizes that the whole darned thing was just a silly misunderstanding. That is all we are going to say about this.

In sports, Super Bowl XVXXLMCMII takes place in Detroit, and, by all accounts, it's a big success for the Motor City, with huge crowds thronging to both of the restaurants. The Pittsburgh Steelers win a game featuring a controversial play in which an apparent Seattle Seahawk touchdown pass is called back after the Steeler defender—in what is later ruled an accident—is gunned down by Vice President Cheney.

But the big sporting event is the Winter Olympics, a glorious, quadrennial celebration of world-class virtuoso athletic accomplishment in sports nobody has ever heard of. Surprise winners include Latvia in the 500-kilometer Modified Nordic Combined; the Republic of Irvingkahnistan in the 2,300-meter Slavic Personified; and U.S. skier Bode Miller in Most

Nike Commercials Featuring a Competitor Who, in the Actual Competitions, Mainly Falls Down.

Speaking of falling, in . . .

MARCH

. . . the real-estate boom appears to be over, as the government reports that, so far in 2006, only one U.S. homeowner managed to sell his house and he had to offer, as an incentive to the buyer, his wife. But the employment numbers remain strong, thanks to strong growth in the sector of people trying to get you to refinance your mortgage for, like, the sixth time. Meanwhile, as the average gasoline price creeps past $2.50, the Hummer company, having downsized from the massive Hummer to the somewhat smaller H2, and then to the even smaller H3, begins development of the H4, which the company says will be "a very rugged skateboard."

In the Academy Awards, the overwhelming favorite for best picture is *Brokeback Mountain*, the story of two men who discover, while spending many isolated weeks together in the mountains, that they enjoy exchanging instant messages with Mark Foley. But in a stunning upset, the Oscar for best picture instead goes to *Crash*, a documentary about Bode Miller.

In other entertainment news, a book by two *San Francisco Chronicle* writers revives suspicions about possible steroid use by San Francisco Giants slugger Barry Bonds, alleging, with extensive documentation, that as recently as ten years ago Bonds was a woman.

In other science news, thrilled NASA astronomers, in what they describe as a "smashing, surprising" discovery, announce that they have found evidence of pockets of water beneath the surface of Enceladus, one of the moons of Saturn, which strongly suggests—as has long been suspected—that astronomers do not get out much.

In foreign news, Israeli voters give a parliamentary majority to acting prime minister Ehud Olmert, because his name can be rearranged to spell HOT EEL DRUM. Meanwhile, in Paris, thousands of demonstrators take to the streets and shut down the city to demonstrate the fact that, hey, it's Paris. In the Middle East, tension mounts in response to mounting tension. We don't know specifically what is happening in Africa, but we know it is bad.

Speaking of things we know are bad, in . . .

APRIL

. . . Tom DeLay decides not to seek reelection to Congress, making the announcement via audiotape from a cave somewhere in Pakistan. Republican leaders express relief over DeLay's decision and issue a statement pledging that there will be "no more Republican scandals, unless somebody finds out about Mark Foley."

Meanwhile, in the Middle East, tension mounts still higher when Iranian president Mahmoud Ahmadinejad announces that Iran has successfully produced enriched uranium, although he claims that his nation plans to use it only for peaceful purposes "such as cooking." In Iraq, there is good news and bad news for the Bush administration. The good news is that rival Iraqi leaders have finally agreed on a new prime minister. The bad news is that it is Nancy Pelosi.

Domestically, the national debate over illegal immigration heats up as thousands of demonstrators take to the streets of major U.S. cities, thus causing a total shutdown of Paris. Meanwhile, the Mexican government, in what is widely

viewed as a deliberate provocation, convenes in Milwaukee. But the big story is the price of gasoline, which continues its relentless climb toward an unprecedented $3 a gallon. Responding quickly, Congress, in a rare display of decisive bipartisan action, takes a recess, with both sides promising to resume bickering the instant they get back.

Speaking of your tax dollars at work, in . . .

MAY

. . . the National Oceanic and Atmospheric Administration, which has a budget of over $3 billion, predicts that the 2006 hurricane season will be worse than usual. This item will seem funnier later in the year. In related news, the voters of New Orleans reelect Ray Nagin as mayor, proving that Hurricane Katrina killed far more brain cells than was previously believed.

On the terrorism front, the Bush administration comes under heavy criticism following press reports that the National Security Agency has been collecting telephone records of millions of Americans. Responding to the outcry, President Bush assures the nation that "the government is not collecting personal information on any individual citizen," adding, "Warren H. Glompett of Boston, call your wife back immediately because your dog has eaten your entire Viagra supply."

In another controversial move, the president announces that he will use National Guard troops to stop illegal immigration. The initial troops are assigned to guard the border between Mexico and Arizona, with California, New Mexico, and Texas being covered by Dick Cheney.

In Houston, former Enron executives Kenneth Lay and Jeffrey Skilling are convicted of fraud by a federal jury, which apparently is not persuaded by the defense's claim that Skilling and Lay could not have been responsible for the collapse of the $100 billion corporation because they were, quote, "both getting haircuts."

True fact: After the verdict, Lay says, "We believe that God, in fact, is in control."

Another true fact: Less than two months later, Lay will die of heart failure.

In sports, Barbaro, the popular racehorse who won the Kentucky Derby, breaks his leg in the Preakness after a freak collision with Bode Miller. Barbaro is forced to retire, although his agent does not rule out future appearances on *Dancing With the Stars*. Meanwhile, the hottest show on TV is the much-hyped finale of *American Idol*, which is won by crooner Taylor Hicks, who narrowly edges out Nancy Pelosi.

Speaking of competition, in . . .

JUNE

. . . the big sports story is the start of the World Cup tournament, with U.S. fans hopeful that our players have finally caught up with the rest of the world in soccer. The American team arrives in Italy brimming with confidence only to be informed that the tournament is being held in Germany. Undaunted, the team boards a train for Geneva, with the coach promising that "we will score many touchdowns."

In politics, the debate over Iraq continues to heat up, with President Bush insisting that "we must stay the course, whatever it may or may not be," while the Democrats claim that they would bring the troops home "immediately," or "in about six months," or "maybe not for a long time," depending on which particular Democrat is speaking and what time of day it is. On a more positive note, U.S. troops kill Abu Musab al-Zarqawi, who is identified by intelligence experts as "a person with a really terrorist-sounding name." In another hopeful development in Iraq, the Sunnis and the Shiites agree to try to come up with a simple way for Americans to remember which one is which.

On the legal front, the Supreme Court rules that the Bush administration cannot try suspected terrorists in ad hoc military tribunals after the court learns that the administration is interpreting "ad hoc" to mean "under water."

Dan Rather, who stopped anchoring the evening news in 2005, announces his retirement from CBS after a career spanning forty-four years and several galaxies. Explaining his decision, Rather cites a desire to "explore other options" and "not keep getting maced by the CBS security guard."

On a happier note, the United States marks the fiftieth anniversary of the Interstate Highway System—an engineering marvel consisting of 47,000 miles of high-speed roads connecting 157,000 Waffle Houses. A formal ceremony is planned but has to be canceled when Dad refuses to stop.

Speaking of speeding while high, in . . .

JULY

. . . the Tour de France bicycle race is once again tainted by suspicions of doping when the winner, American Floyd Landis, is clocked ascending the Alps at over two hundred miles per hour. Landis denies that he uses illegal drugs, attributing his performance to, quote, "gears."

In other sports highlights, Italy defeats France in a World Cup final match that is marred by a violent head-butting incident involving Bode Miller. The U.S. team fares poorly in the World Cup, failing to win a single match; the players blame this on their inability to adjust to the "no hands" rule.

But the month's big story occurs in the Middle East, where violence flares along the Israel-Lebanon border in response to the fact that, because of terrible planning, the two countries are located right next to each other. In another troubling international development, rogue state North Korea test-fires seven ballistic missiles, including two believed to be potentially capable of reaching U.S. soil. World tension goes back down when the missiles, upon reaching an altitude of two hundred feet, explode and spell HAPPY BIRTHDAY. American military analysts caution that these missiles "could easily be modified to spell something more threatening."

In other rocket news, the troubled U.S. space program suffers yet another setback when the launch of the shuttle *Discovery* is delayed for several days by Transportation Security Administration screeners, who insist that the astronauts remove their shoes before they go through the metal detector. Finally, however, *Discovery* blasts off and flies a flawless mission, highlighted by scientific experiments proving when you let go of things in space, they float around, same as last year.

Outer space remains in the news in . . .

AUGUST

. . . when the International Astronomical Union rules that Pluto will no longer be classified as a major planet on the grounds that it is "less than half the size of James Gandolfini." A top U.S. law firm immediately files a class action lawsuit on behalf of Pluto, as well as "anybody else who has been hurt by this ruling or has ever experienced neck pain."

In sports, a French medical laboratory burns to the ground following the catastrophic explosion of Floyd Landis's urine sample.

Fidel Castro is rumored to be seriously ill following publication of photographs showing worms crawling out of his

eye sockets. Cuban authorities insist that the aging leader is merely recovering from surgery and that for the time being government operations are in the capable hands of Nancy Pelosi.

As the situation in Lebanon deteriorates, Secretary of State Condoleezza Rice warns that if violence continues, the United States will have no choice but to dispatch Vice President Cheney to the region to hunt quail. Within minutes, a cease-fire breaks out, with both sides agreeing to resume fire at a mutually convenient future date.

Meanwhile, commercial air travel turns into a total nightmare. No, wait, it was already a total nightmare. But it turns into an even worse total nightmare after Britain uncovers a terrorist plot targeting international flights, which results in a whole new set of security rules, including a total ban on all gels and liquids, including spit, urine, heavy perspirers, and lactating women. After days of chaos at the airports, the TSA issues a new directive stating that "Passengers may carry small quantities of liquids on board, but only if they are inside clear, one-quart, sealable plastic bags." This leads to still more chaos as many TSA employees interpret this to mean that the *passengers* must be inside the bags. Eventually, the TSA issues a clarification stating that "If necessary, the bags can have airholes."

Elsewhere in the War on Terror, the Bush administration suffers a setback when a federal judge in Michigan rules that U.S. authorities cannot call up suspected terrorists and try to get them to switch long-distance carriers.

In crime news, a man in Thailand claims that he had something to do with the 1996 murder of JonBenét Ramsey. It quickly becomes clear that the man is an unstable creep whose story is totally unbelievable, so the cable TV shows drop it.

Ha-ha! Just kidding! The cable TV shows go into days of round-the-clock, All JonBenét All the Time Wallow Mode. Battalions of legal experts are brought in, some of them so excited at the opportunity to revisit the JonBenét tragedy that additional janitors have to be brought into the studios to mop up puddles of expert weewee.

On the weather front, the until-now-quiet hurricane season erupts in fearsome fury in the form of Tropical Storm Ernesto, which hurricane experts, using scientific computer models, predict could become a major storm and inflict devastation upon Texas, or possibly Florida, or Connecticut. A state of near panic sets in as millions of coastal residents jam gas stations, hardware stores, and supermarkets, while many schools and businesses close. Tension mounts for days until finally Ernesto slams into Florida with all the fury of a diseased fruit fly. Life slowly returns to normal for everyone except the ever-vigilant hurricane experts, who immediately begin scanning their scientific computer simulations for the next potentially deadly threat.

And speaking of deadly, in . . .

SEPTEMBER

. . . Steve "Crocodile Hunter" Irwin, filming an underwater episode of a TV show, is fatally wounded when—in what biologists describe as a freak accident—he collides with Bode Miller. Meanwhile, Americans—already on edge because of concern over terrorism, avian flu, AIDS, nuclear escalation, and global warming—find themselves facing a deadly new menace: killer spinach. The lethal vegetable is removed from supermarket shelves by police SWAT teams; many units of innocent produce are harmed. Paris shuts down completely.

Speaking of vegetables, the United States Congress is rocked by yet another scandal with the publication of e-mails and instant messages sent to male pages by Congressman Mark Foley of Florida in which he explicitly discusses acts of a sheepherding nature. As the scandal expands, House Republican leaders issue a statement claiming that they "are not aware of any so-called Congressman Mark Foley of Florida." Democrats cite Foley as another example of Republican corruption, declaring that they would never, ever, under any circumstances, tolerate such behavior, unless it involved a consenting page.

In other political developments, *The New York Times* prints a leaked top secret government report expressing doubts about the war in Iraq. The Bush administration holds a secret meeting to prepare a response, but within hours the *Times* prints leaked details of the meeting, including who went to the bathroom and why. The administration then attempts to take out the *Times* building with a missile, but the *Times,* using leaked launch codes, redirects it to the *Washington Post.* As the debate over Iraq heats up, President Bush pledges to "keep on continuing to stay the present course while at the same time not doing anything different." Democratic leaders declare that they have a "bold new plan" for Iraq, which they will reveal just as soon as *The New York Times* leaks it to them.

Abroad, Pope Benedict XVI gets in big trouble when he gives a speech suggesting that the Muslim religion has historically been linked to violence. Ha-ha! What a crazy idea! The pope soon sees that he has made a big mistake and apologizes several times.

Rumors about Fidel Castro's health continue to swirl following publication of a photograph showing Venezuelan president Hugo Chávez shaking Castro's hand. The rest of Castro's body is nowhere to be seen.

Speaking of the Communist Menace, in . . .

OCTOBER

. . . North Korea conducts an underground nuclear test, which is especially troubling because the ground in question is located in Wyoming. This goes virtually unnoticed in Washington, where everybody continues to be obsessed with the growing body of instant messages generated by Mark Foley, who, despite his busy schedule as a lawmaker, apparently found time to attempt to become sheepherding buddies with pretty much every young male in North America.

In other political developments, Sen. Barack Obama, looking back on a career in the U.S. Senate that spans nearly twenty months, allows as how he might be ready to move on to the presidency. Obamamania sweeps the nation as millions of voters find themselves deeply impressed by Obama's views, and the fact that he was on *Oprah*. In a gracious gesture from a potential 2008 rival, Sen. Hillary Clinton sends Obama a goodluck card, which is stapled to the head of a horse.

Opponents of illegal Mexican immigration cheer when Congress authorizes the construction of a seven-hundred-mile fence. Their cheers quickly fade when they learn that because of wording inserted at the last minute by senators Robert Byrd and Ted Stevens, 650 miles of the fence will be constructed in West Virginia and Alaska.

Vice President Dick Cheney again becomes the center of controversy when, appearing on a radio show, he defends the interrogation technique known as "waterboarding" as a legitimate antiterrorism tool, not torture. At first, the host disagrees, but after several "commercial breaks" Dick brings him around.

A strong earthquake shocks Hawaii, causing Paris to shut down completely.

In sports, a football game between the University of Miami and Florida International University is marred by violence, prompting both schools to seriously consider banning players from carrying handguns onto the field. In baseball, the New York Yankees, despite being clearly the best and most expensive team the world has ever seen, fail to even get into the World Series, leaving Yankee fans to spend yet another bitter off-season wondering why their team can't simply be awarded the championship and not have to play these stupid games against clearly inferior teams from dirtball cities that don't even have subways.

But October ends on a happy note with the celebration of Halloween, a night of magical fun when millions of youngsters, all over America, are kept indoors. The most popular costumes this year, according to retailers, are Power Ranger and Nancy Pelosi.

As the election approaches, polls show that the Democrats have a good chance to regain control of Congress. But then disaster strikes in the form of John "Mr. Laffs" Kerry, who, addressing a college audience, attempts to tell a joke, which is like a fish attempting to play the piano. This has major repercussions in . . .

NOVEMBER

. . . when Kerry's "joke" causes widespread outrage, prompting Kerry, with typical humility, to insist that it was obviously humorous and anybody who disagrees is an idiot. Kerry is finally subdued by Democratic strategists armed with duct tape, but not before many political analysts see a tightening of the race to control Congress.

As the campaign lumbers to the finish line, the Republicans desperately hope that the voters will not notice that they— once the party of small government—have turned into the party of war-bungling, corruption-tolerating, pork-spewing, power-lusting toads, while the Democrats desperately hope that the voters will not notice that they are still, basically, the Democrats. The actual voters, of course, are paying no attention, having given up on politics months ago because every time they turn on the TV all they see are political ads accusing pretty much every candidate on either side of being, at minimum, a child molester.

Thus nobody really knows what will happen as the voters go to the polls. In Florida, nobody knows anything even after the voting is over, because—prepare to be shocked—many electronic balloting machines malfunction. Voters in one district report that their machines, instead of displaying the candidates for Congress, showed *Star Wars IV.* (By an overwhelming margin, this district elects Jabba the Hutt.)

Nationwide, however, it eventually becomes clear that the Democrats have gained control of both houses of Congress. President Bush handles the defeat with surprisingly good humor, possibly because his staff has not told him about it. For their part, future House Speaker Nancy Pelosi and future Senate Majority Leader Harry Reid issue a joint statement promising to "make every effort to find common ground with the president," adding: "We are clearly lying." Pelosi sets about the difficult task of trying to fill leadership posts with Democrats who have not been videotaped discussing bribes with federal undercover agents.

The first major casualty of the GOP defeat is Defense Secretary Donald Rumsfeld, who, the day after the election, is invited to go quail hunting with the vice president. He is never seen again. As Rumsfeld's replacement, the president nominates—in what is widely seen as a change in direction on Iraq—Barbra Streisand.

In other celebrity news, Michael Richards, a graduate of the Mel Gibson School of Stand-Up, responds to a comedy club heckler by unleashing a racist tirade so vile that even John Kerry realizes it is not funny. A chastened Richards apologizes for his behavior, citing, by way of explanation, the fact that he is a moron.

Speaking of which, O.J. Simpson is once again in the headlines when Fox TV announces that Simpson will be interviewed on a two-night special show in conjunction with his new book, *If I Did It,* in which he will explain how, "hypothetically," he would have murdered Nicole Brown Simpson and Ronald Goldman. This idea is so sick, so disgusting, so utterly depraved, that it would undoubtedly get huge ratings. But Fox, faced with withering criticism, is forced to cancel the project, which is the brainchild of publisher Judith Regan, about whom you could write a "hypothetical" book titled *If Judith Regan Had the Moral Standards of a Tapeworm.*

On the economic front, the holiday shopping season officially kicks off with "Black Friday" and retailers are pleased with the numbers: 2,038 shoppers hospitalized, up 37 percent from last year.

In other good news, with four days left in the virtually storm-free 2006 hurricane season and still no storms in sight, U.S. weather experts, citing new data, predict that the season will end up having been very mild. This forecast turns out to be right on the money, but the experts waste no time on self-congratulation as they immediately begin making scientific predictions for next year's hurricane season, which, they warn, could be a bad one.

Speaking of bad . . .

DECEMBER

. . . gets off to a troubling start with the worsening situation in Iraq worsening faster than ever. The nation's hopes for a solution are pinned on the Iraq Study Group, a presidentially appointed blue-ribbon panel consisting of five Republicans, five Democrats, and the Wizard of Oz. In accordance with long-standing Washington tradition, the panel first formally leaks its report to *The New York Times,* then delivers it to the president, who turns it over to White House personnel specially trained in reading things.

In essence, the study group recommends a three-pronged approach, consisting of (1) a gradual withdrawal of U.S. troops, but not on a fixed timetable, (2) intensified training of Iraqi troops, and (3) the physical relocation of Iraq, including buildings, to Greenland. Republican and Democratic leaders, after considering the report for the better part of a nanosecond, commence what is expected to be a minimum of two more years of bickering.

With the Iraq situation pretty much solved, the world's attention shifts to Iran and its suspected nuclear program, which becomes the subject of renewed concern after U.S. satellites detect a glowing four-hundred-foot-high spider striding around Tehran. Iranian President Mahmoud Ahmadinejad insists that it is "a peaceful spider" that will be used "only for mail delivery." Shortly thereafter, North Korea—in what many observers see as a deliberate provocation—detonates a nuclear device inside the Lincoln Memorial.

Finally responding to these new threats to international stability, the five permanent members of the UN Security Council—the U.S., the U.K., Russia, China, and Google—hold an emergency meeting in Paris, where, after heated debate, they vote to have a bottle of 1959 Château Margaux with their entrée. Unfortunately, they cannot agree on a dessert wine, causing the city, which had just reopened, to shut down completely.

In other food news, New York City, having apparently solved all of its other problems, bans "trans fats." Hours later, police surround a Burger King in Brooklyn and fire fifty-seven bullets into a man suspected of carrying a concealed Whopper. The medical examiner's office, after a thorough investigation, concludes that the man "definitely could have developed artery problems down the road."

Speaking of health problems, rumors that Fidel Castro is ailing gain new strength when, at an official state dinner in Havana, a waiter accidentally tips over the longtime Cuban leader's urn, spilling most of him on the floor.

In other deceased-communist news, British police decide to treat the mysterious death of a former Russian spy in London as a murder, caused by the radioactive element polonium-210. New York immediately bans the element, forcing the closure of 70 percent of the city's Taco Bells.

As the year, finally, nears its conclusion, Americans turn their attention to the holiday season, which they celebrate— as generations have before them—by frantically overbidding on eBay for the Sony PlayStation 3, of which Sony, anticipating the near-homicidal level of demand, manufactured an estimated eleven units. Millions of Americans also head "home for the holidays," making this one of the busiest air travel seasons ever. The always-vigilant TSA responds by raising the Color Code Security Status to "Ultraviolet," which means that passengers may not board an airplane if they contain blood.

But despite the well-founded fear of terrorism, the seemingly unbreakable and escalating cycle of violence in the Middle East, the uncertain world economic future, the menace of global warming, the near certainty that rogue states run by lunatics will soon have nuclear weapons, and the fact that America is confronting these dangers with a federal government sharply divided into two hostile parties unable to agree on anything except that the other side is scum, Americans face the new year with a remarkable lack of worry, and for a very good reason: They are busy drinking beer and watching football.

So Happy New Year.

(Burp!)

2007

AMERICA TAKES A STANCE

It was a year that strode boldly into the stall of human events and took a wide stance astride the porcelain bowl of history.

It was a year in which roughly 17,000 leading presidential contenders, plus of course Dennis Kucinich, held roughly 63,000 debates, during which they spewed out roughly 153 trillion words; and yet the only truly memorable phrase emitted in any political context was, "Don't tase me, bro!"

It was a year filled with bizarre, insane, destructive behavior, an alarming amount of which involved astronauts.

In short, 2007 was a year of deep gloom, pierced occasionally by rays of even deeper gloom. Oh, sure, there were a few bright spots:

- Several courageous members of the U.S. Congress—it could be as many as a dozen—decided, incredibly, *not* to run for president.

- O. J. Simpson discovered that, although you might be able to avoid jail time for committing a double homicide, the justice system draws the line at attempted theft of sports memorabilia.

- Toward the end of the year, entire days went by when it was possible to not think about Paris Hilton.

- Apple released the iPhone, which, as we understand it, enables users to fly, cure cancer, read minds, and travel through time.

- The plucky, lovable New York Yankees once again found a way, against all odds, to bring joy to the literally billions of people who do not root for them.

- Dick Cheney did not shoot anybody, as far as we know.

But other than that, 2007 was a disaster. American consumers came to fear products manufactured in China, which covers pretty much everything in the typical American home except the dirt. Global warming continued to worsen, despite the efforts of leading climate experts such as Madonna and Leonardo DiCaprio, who emerged briefly from their private jets to give the rest of us helpful tips on reducing our carbon footprints.

On the economic front, the dollar continued to lose value against all major foreign currencies and most brands of bath-

room tissue. There was a major collapse in the credit market, caused by the fact that for most of this decade, every other radio commercial has been some guy selling mortgages to people who clearly should not have mortgages. ("No credit? No job? On death row? No problem!") It got so bad that you couldn't let your dog run loose, because it would come home with a mortgage. The subprime-mortgage fiasco resulted in huge stock-market losses, and the executives responsible, under the harsh rules of Wall Street justice, were forced to accept lucrative retirement packages.

So they did OK. But for the rest of us, it was another bad year. And as is so often true of bad years, it began with . . .

JANUARY

. . . when Democrats, having won the November election, take control of both houses of Congress with surprisingly little loss of life. In the House of Representatives, incoming Speaker Nancy Pelosi pledges "a new era of bipartisan cooperation," then brings the gavel down on the head of outgoing Speaker Dennis Hastert.

Upon taking power, the Democrats, who campaigned vigorously against the war in Iraq, and who hailed their victory as a clear voter mandate to get the troops out of Iraq, immediately get down to the business of being careful not to do anything that might actually result in the removal of troops from Iraq, in case that might turn out to be a bad idea. This is fine with President Bush, who calls for a "troop surge," based on his understanding of the comprehensive Iraq Study Group Report, as interpreted for him by aides equipped with 20,000 G.I. Joe action figures.

As the debate over Iraq intensifies, the eyes of a worried nation turn to another trouble spot: New York City, where Donald Trump and Rosie O'Donnell are locked in a bitter high-stakes battle to determine who is the bigger horse's ass. After meeting with both sides, a visibly shaken Secretary of State Condoleezza Rice reports that Trump's hair "is exactly the same color as a Cheez-It." While the White House ponders its options, congressional Democrats vow to strongly op-

BLAM BLAM
RAT-TAT-TAT
EAT LEAD,
INSURGENT!

pose whatever action the president decides to take, while at the same time voting to fund it.

On the Homeland Security front, the U.S. government begins requiring people arriving in the U.S. by air from Mexico or Canada to present passports, fueling speculation that Canada is a foreign country. The government notes that the passport requirement "does not apply to people sneaking in by land."

The slump in home sales continues into the new year, with a total, nationwide, of one home sold in January. In many cities, gangs of real estate agents—sometimes wearing "colors" in the form of canary-yellow jackets—roam the streets, surrounding their victims and extracting money from them in forcible "closings."

In sports, a Los Angeles team signs glamorous British soccer star David Beckham to a $250 million contract. This raises eyebrows, both because of the amount of money, and because the team is the Dodgers. But Beckham's glamorous presence quickly boosts ticket sales; within days the Lakers sign Angelina Jolie.

Sports remains in the news in . . .

FEBRUARY

. . . when South Florida hosts Super Bowl Roman Numeral. Because of concern over terrorism, security is extremely tight, particularly outside South Beach nightclubs, where large bouncers refuse to let any terrorists inside unless they are really hot. After what feels like three months of pregame festivities, an actual game is played, pitting the Chicago Bears against the Indianapolis Peyton Mannings. What begins as a close contest is broken wide open in the third quarter when the Bears' defense is unable to stop a 1993 Buick LeSabre driven by 87-year-old North Miami Beach resident Winifred Bingleman, who took a wrong turn on her way to Mah-Jongg. She is immediately signed by the Miami Dolphins.

In other February action, Democrats in the House of Representatives, after a large amount of talking, pass a non-binding resolution sternly ordering President Bush to get out of Iraq, unless of course he chooses not to. Over in the Senate,

Democrats try to pass a nonbinding resolution that would not have bound the president to the same course of action that the House resolution did not bind him to. But that one fails, leaving the president, according to political observers, somewhat less nonbound than he might otherwise have been. Everyone agrees it has been a busy, busy time in Washington.

Abroad, the Six-Party Talks in Beijing conclude on an optimistic note as North Korea's leader, Insane Lunatic Liar-il, announces that his country will dismantle its nuclear-weapons program just as soon as it receives the nuclear dismantler that it ordered on eBay. All six parties agree that this sounds reasonable; they resume partying. On a more ominous nuclear note, President Bush warns Iran that it is, quote, "awfully close to Iraq, if you look at a map, which I have." In another increasingly tense international arena, the UN Security Council sends 1,000 peacekeeping troops to New York City in an effort to quell Rosie O'Donnell, who repels them by shouting.

But the big news in February is the death and subsequent wacky adventures of Anna Nicole Smith, whose body remains in a refrigerator in the medical examiner's office while her infant child is embroiled in a paternity dispute that eventually comes to involve pretty much every adult male resident of the United States except Richard Simmons. The news media cover this story with their usual taste and restraint, keeping the public informed of important developments via such journalistic innovations as the Refrigerator Cam; Greta Van Susteren jets to Aruba in case there is a Natalee Holloway link. The dramatic finale takes place in a Florida courtroom presided over by Judge Weeping Twit, who, in a display of Solomonic wisdom, rules that everyone involved will get a TV show.

Another important February story getting huge media coverage is "Revenge of the Scary Astronaut Diaper Woman," which concerns astronaut Lisa Nowak, who, after allegedly driving nonstop from Houston to the Orlando International Airport, is arrested and charged with the attempted murder of a woman whom she viewed as a rival for a male astronaut, who no doubt wishes he had just stayed up there in space. According to the police, Nowak's car contained latex gloves, a black wig, a BB pistol, a knife, pepper spray and—most disturbing of all—a 55-gallon drum filled with Tang.

In other aviation news, JetBlue has a public-relations disaster when ten of its flights are stranded on runways for so long that they are enveloped by glaciers. Fortunately, all the passengers manage to survive, in some cases by eating their carry-on luggage. This fiasco prompts the FAA to fine JetBlue for violating strict federal regulations against allowing passengers to have anything edible in coach class.

In the Academy Awards, Martin Scorsese finally breaks his long drought, winning a best-picture Oscar for his film *Give Me an Oscar or This Time I Swear I Will Kill Myself.*

Speaking of drama, in . . .

MARCH

. . . the riveting trial of Scooter "Scooter" Libby, former chief of staff to Vice President Dick Cheney, concludes with Scooter being convicted on federal charges of being guilty of something having to do with Nigeria and somebody named Valerie, but we are darned if we can remember what, although we certainly hope Scooter has learned his lesson.

In other scandal news, Attorney General Alberto Gonzales gets into hot water when congressional Democrats allege that his name can be rearranged to spell RE-LABEL ZOO GNATS and GALA LOBSTER ZONE. President Bush calls Gonzales "a person in which I have the utmost whaddycallit" and pledges to "stand behind him 100 percent for the time being."

Speaking of time: Americans attempt to adjust to a new daylight saving time law, which Congress passed because it apparently felt that the old law was not annoying and confusing enough. The new law produces immediate economic benefits in the form of an estimated $175 billion paid by corporations and individuals to fix the computers, PDAs, phone systems, etc., that were screwed up by the time change. Of course, none of this affects Congress, which has exempted itself from the new law and continues to operate by sundial.

On a somber note, Anna Nicole Smith is finally laid to rest in the Bahamas in an intimate funeral service attended only by family, close friends, acquaintances, total strangers, tourists, and an estimated 750 cable TV legal analysts, several of whom have to be forcibly removed from the casket as they attempt to commit one final act of legal analysis.

Speaking of bad taste, in . . .

APRIL

. . . the broadcasting industry is shocked, shocked, when radio personality Don Imus, who has spent several decades making and chuckling at crude racist statements, makes a crude racist statement about the Rutgers women's basketball team. The Reverends Jesse Jackson and Al Sharpton are deeply offended and immediately set about the difficult but necessary work of drawing still more attention to themselves. Before it is over, everybody involved will be wealthier, except, of course, the members of the Rutgers women's basketball team.

In politics, the burgeoning Alberto Gonzales scandal—rapidly becoming the most riveting scandal to rivet Washington since the "Scooter" Libby scandal—burgeons still further when congressional Democrats charge that Gonzales's name can also be rearranged to spell A STERN LEGAL BOZO and SNOT BLAZE GALORE. President Bush defends his beleaguered attorney general, accusing the Democrats of "a new low in beleaguering" and stating that he has "no intention whatsoever of replacing Mr. Gonzales with anybody else, such as Michael Mukasey, if he is available."

Speaking of beleaguered: Rosie O'Donnell announces that she will leave the TV show *The View* to pursue a career making bizarre statements on the Internet. Although O'Donnell claims her departure is amicable, insiders say she tried to oust Barbara Walters as the show's producer, a move that Walters was able to repel by blasting the outspoken comedienne with 150,000 cubic feet of hair spray, which for Barbara is nearly a two-day supply.

In other show business news, the surprise contestant on *American Idol* is llama-hairstyled Sanjaya Malakar, who, with the support of millions of viewers, all apparently deaf, manages to reach the late rounds of the competition before being eliminated by a blowgun dart from Simon Cowell. Upon being revived, Sanjaya is signed by the Miami Dolphins.

Another surprise hit in April—in fact, the number one recording, played relentlessly for days by every radio and TV station in the country—is "Alec Baldwin Talks to His Eleven-Year-Old Daughter the Way Tony Soprano Talks to Somebody Whose Legs He Is About to Drive Over in His Chevrolet Suburban."

Speaking of strong action, in . . .

MAY

. . . Democrats in Congress—continuing to implement their policy of being passionately against the war, while avoiding doing anything that might get them blamed for stopping the war—vote to continue funding the war, but boldly enter many snippy remarks about it into the Congressional Record. President Bush receives this devastating news stoically, then goes ahead and makes his putt.

Meanwhile the Senate, after months of secret negotiations, releases its comprehensive immigration reform plan, under which immigrants would earn points toward becoming U.S. citizens by having basic citizenship skills such as being able to do the Electric Slide and place an order at Starbucks. To placate conservatives, the plan also calls for a three-hundred-mile fence to be constructed around Rosie O'Donnell.

In presidential politics, Florida—continuing its proud tradition of screwing up elections—announces that it will move its primary up to January 29. This infuriates Iowa and New Hampshire, which want to be first because otherwise no sane person would ever go to either state in the winter. So New Hampshire moves its primary to early January, and Iowa moves its caucus to even earlier in January. Soon the other states, not wanting to be left out, start moving up *their* elections; before the frenzy is over, Nebraska has officially declared that its 2008 primary election will take place in 1973. Of course, normal American voters pay no attention to any of this, which is why they are always the last ones to find out who their presidential choices will be.

Abroad, the French presidential election, in what political analysts see as a break with recent trends, is won by John Kerry.

As May draws to a close and the Atlantic hurricane season looms, weather experts, having reviewed all their data and their sophisticated computer models, announce that they have absolutely no clue what is going to happen.

Ha-ha! We are, of course, kidding. The experts confidently predict that we are going to have a worse-than-usual hurricane season. This is also what they confidently predicted last year, which, as you may recall, was an unusually quiet season. It is only a matter of time before these experts are hired by the Miami Dolphins.

In sports, the Indianapolis 500 is won by Britney Spears in a car equipped with two infants but no car seats.

Speaking of outstanding drivers, in . . .

JUNE

. . . the nation is riveted by the drama of Paris Hilton, who, after a string of motor-vehicle violations including driving with a suspended license, driving at excessive speed through a nightclub, driving over the young of an endangered species, and driving with the brain functionality of a cabbage, is ordered to go to jail, then is released from jail, and then—in what many observers see as an unfair punishment, based solely on resentment of her celebrity status—is burned at the stake.

No, seriously: Paris is sent back to prison for several brutal weeks, during which she is repeatedly subjected to a harsh generic hair conditioner. Somehow she survives this ordeal and, upon leaving prison, adopts a low public profile, except for appearing with Larry King, who does a fine job once he realizes, about forty minutes into the interview, that she is not Goldie Hawn.

In other June TV highlights:

- Cuban television broadcasts an interview of Fidel Castro, apparently intended to prove that the ailing dictator is still alive; cynics note, however, that the interview was conducted by Edward R. Murrow.
- The hit HBO series *The Sopranos* comes to an ambiguous end when, in midscene, the screen goes black. Many viewers at first think this is a technical problem; cable TV companies log three million complaint calls, nearly 30 percent of them from the White House.

In other government action, the U.S. Senate discovers that its comprehensive immigration reform bill, despite having been painstakingly crafted behind closed doors by veteran bill-crafters, is unpopular with a segment of the U.S. population defined as "the public." The Senate responds swiftly, dropping the immigration issue like a bag of rat sputum and returning to its traditional role of funding large unnecessary projects in West Virginia named after Robert Byrd.

In sports, the Anaheim Ducks defeat the Ottawa Senators

in a Stanley Cup play-off series watched, worldwide, by most of the players' parents.

But the biggest story in June, as well as the history of the universe, is the release of the Apple iPhone, which, in addition to enabling you to make phone calls, has all kinds of brilliant and innovative features, including AutoFondle, an application that enables the iPhone to fondle itself during those times when you are unable to fondle it manually because you're sleeping or undergoing surgery from wounds you sustained when friends or coworkers finally lost it and beat you senseless to make you shut up about your freaking iPhone already.

Speaking of medical procedures, in . . .

JULY

. . . President Bush undergoes a colonoscopy; congressional Democrats immediately pass a resolution condemning the procedure, while maintaining that they "fully support the colonoscope." Vice President Cheney serves as acting president for two and a half hours, during which he performs what his office describes as "routine executive duties," including "signing some routine papers" and "ordering some routine bomb strikes against Iran." France immediately surrenders.

In other executive action, President Bush, on the eve of July Fourth, commutes "Scooter" Libby's prison sentence on the grounds that, quote, "Hey, c'mon, it's Scooter." Congressional Democrats are outraged, but the public is more concerned with the issue of whether to go ahead and have that fifth beer.

Speaking of which: The troubled space program is dealt yet another blow when a special panel reveals that on at least two occasions, astronauts were cleared to fly while drunk. This is thought to explain some unusual research conducted by shuttle crews, including the "weightless naked Twister experiment" and "wedgies in space."

On the environmental front, the big story is Al Gore's Live Earth, a massive rock concert in which more than 150 musical acts perform at eleven locations around the world to fight global warming, which is swiftly brought to its knees.

In the arts, July is dominated by the release of the seventh and last Harry Potter book, *Harry Potter Spends Half the Book Camping*, which enthralls the nation as nothing has enthralled it since the release of the iPhone. The book is generally well received, although some fans are troubled by the ending, which culminates in the death of Harry's longtime nemesis, Tony Soprano.

In sports, suspicions of doping continue to plague the Tour de France when the grueling 2,200-mile race is won, in a stunning upset, by Barry Bonds. Pro basketball also suffers a blow following reports that NBA referee Tim Donaghy bet on games that he officiated; which could explain some of his questionable calls in critical situations, including fouls for "bad posture" and "dribbling too loud."

Speaking of image problems, in . . .

AUGUST

. . . Mattel, responding to new reports of hazardous materials in Chinese-made products, recalls millions of toys. A Mattel spokesperson insists that "there is no cause for alarm," but suggests that consumers who have come into contact with the

Barbie Magic Kitty Dream Castle should "seek medical help" and "try not to breathe on anyone."

In politics, the leading Democratic and Republican contenders for president, having failed to draw much of an audience for their previous debates, experiment with new formats. The Republicans hold a "Charades Debate," during which Mike Huckabee injures his shoulder attempting to mime his plan for tax reform; the Democrats fare little better in their "West Side Story Rumble Debate," which ends early when a switchblade-wielding John Edwards "accidentally" stabs Hillary Clinton in her pantsuit. Despite the excitement, both debates get lower TV ratings than a rerun of the Ducks-Senators Stanley Cup final.

But the big story in politics is Idaho's Senator Larry "Wide Stance" Craig, who pleads guilty in August after being arrested in June for allegedly attempting to engage in acts of explicit filibustering with an undercover detective in a Minneapolis airport bathroom stall. Senator Craig explains that, even though he pled guilty, he is innocent, but he promises that he will resign, a pledge he later clarifies by explaining that he will not resign. The Senate, responding with unusual speed and firmness, funds a large, unnecessary project in Alaska named after Ted Stevens.

In other scandal news, beleaguered Attorney General Alberto Gonzales is finally forced to resign when Democrats leak documents showing that his name can also be rearranged to spell LARGE OZONE BLAST and GLEAN ZEBRA STOOL. President

Bush attempts to commute Gonzales's sentence, only to be informed that there isn't one.

On the weather front, the nation is gripped by a heat wave. This has happened pretty much every August since the dawn of human civilization, but it totally stuns the news media.

In show business, Merv Griffin, entrepreneur, entertainer, and host, passes away at age eighty-two and appears for two riveting hours on *Larry King Live*.

In sports, Barry Bonds, fresh off his Tour de France triumph, hits his record-breaking 756th home run in front of a crowd that does not include baseball commissioner Bud Selig, who had this other thing he had to do. In Cooperstown, New York, the National Baseball Hall of Fame starts making plans for a special Barry Bonds Wing, to be located in Taiwan.

But the big sports story is Michael Vick, whose guilty plea in connection with a dogfighting operation effectively ends his football career, costing him a fortune and setting a standard for moronic, immoral, and self-destructive professional-athlete behavior that will take O. J. Simpson nearly a month to surpass.

Speaking of troubled personalities, in . . .

SEPTEMBER

. . . Iranian President Mahmoud "Scooter" Ahmadinejad, speaking at Columbia University, defends his denial of the

Holocaust and claims there are no gays in Iran. He and his entourage then head to Greenwich Village to shop for chaps.

In Washington, Congress once again tackles Iraq as General David Petraeus and Ambassador Ryan Crocker testify in Senate and House committee hearings totaling sixteen hours, of which eleven hours are taken up by Joe Biden's welcoming remarks. Afterward, Democrats and Republicans agree that they have gained a better understanding of this extremely complex issue and will henceforth abandon crude partisanship and try to find common ground on the planet Floob, where this might actually happen. Here on Earth, both sides immediately resume declaring that the other side is scum.

President Bush nominates Michael B. Mukasey to be attorney general, despite published reports that his name can be rearranged to spell LUBE MAMA'S HICKEY and MACE HIS LEAKY BUM. Senate leaders, in a rare display of bipartisanship, pledge to fund large, unnecessary projects in both West Virginia *and* Alaska.

A talk by John Kerry at the University of Florida is interrupted by a struggle between police and a disruptive student, who shouts "Don't tase me, bro!" at an officer, who then tasers him, possibly because she is not, in fact, a "bro." The video of this incident—showing the student shouting "Help!" and wrestling with police on the floor while Kerry's droning voice can be heard in the background saying "It's a very important question"—becomes a huge YouTube hit. The consensus is that the student was obnoxious, although the ACLU objects to the tasering, arguing that, quote, "You get better results with pepper spray."

In other political developments:

- Fred Thompson, ending months of speculation, formally declares that he has a hot wife.
- Hillary Clinton's campaign returns $850,000 in contributions raised by fugitive Chinese-American businessman Norman Hsu following published reports that the money had a high lead content.

In Las Vegas, O. J. Simpson, an ordinary citizen minding his own business and exercising his basic constitutional right to retrieve sports memorabilia from somebody else's hotel room with the aid of armed thugs, somehow runs afoul of the law. He insists he is innocent, but winds up facing trial on robbery and kidnapping charges that could send him to jail for a life term, after which he will undoubtedly be signed by the Miami Dolphins.

Speaking of trouble, in . . .

OCTOBER

. . . uncontrolled fires sweep across large areas of California. President Bush, looking down from his helicopter, pronounces the scene "devastating," only to be informed that the helicopter is flying over Camp David. Aides later explain that the president meant "devastating in a good way." Congress, after an intense debate, narrowly passes a nonbinding resolution supporting the firefighters.

In politics, the race for the Democratic nomination heats up during a nationally televised debate when John Edwards and Barack Obama, in what political observers view as a thinly veiled attack on Hillary Clinton, repeatedly raise the issue of ankle size. On the Republican side, Sam Brownback announces that he is dropping out of the race; political observers view this as an indication that he thought he was in the race.

Al Gore is named cowinner of the Nobel Peace Prize for his efforts to raise awareness of climate change. In an emotional statement, Gore says he is "deeply humbled," stressing that he could not have won the honor without "an extremely high IQ."

On the economic front, the Federal Reserve Board cuts interest rates in an effort to counteract economic stagnation caused by the fact that Americans are now spending $743 billion a year—nearly half their disposable income – on Hannah Montana tickets.

In aviation news, the Airbus A380, the world's largest passenger plane, makes its maiden commercial flight from Singapore to Sydney. In full economy configuration, the giant plane carries 853 passengers, a crew of 20, and 3 packages of pretzels.

In sports, track star Marion Jones admits that she used

SEN. ALBUS "LARRY"
DUMBLEDORE
R-IDAHO

banned substances. She is stripped of her five Olympic medals by the International Olympic Committee and hired as a designated hitter by the San Francisco Giants.

In entertainment news, author J. K. Rowling surprises fans of the *Harry Potter* series when she reveals that Albus Dumbledore, headmaster of Hogwarts School, was also, secretly, a United States senator from Idaho.

October ends with America shutting down for roughly a week to celebrate Halloween, a time when millions of adults get back in touch with their "inner child" by getting drunk while dressed as pimps and hookers. For younger children there is also trick-or-treating, but because of safety concerns this is pretty much restricted to Kansas.

Speaking of pimps and hookers, in . . .

NOVEMBER

. . . the presidential contenders start to show signs of emotional wear during their debates, as exemplified by Mitt Romney's decision, following a heated exchange on trade policy, to whip out a Sharpie and write a bad word on Rudy Giuliani's forehead. The mood is equally testy on the Democratic side, where Bill Richardson, in the role of peacekeeper, has to physically restrain Hillary Clinton from repeatedly striking Barack Obama with Dennis Kucinich.

Meanwhile CNN faces allegations of allowing planted questions in its televised debates after a group of audience members billed as "ordinary, undecided voters"—including a police officer, a construction worker, a soldier, a rancher, and a Native American—turn out to be, in fact, the Village People.

As the political debates increase in frequency and intensity, the American public, realizing that the time to make a decision will soon be at hand, tunes in by the millions to the finale of *Dancing with the Stars*. The surprise winner is race-car driver Helio Castroneves, who is immediately signed by the Miami Dolphins.

In economic news, the Federal Reserve Board, responding

to recession fears and the continued weakening of the dollar, votes unanimously to be paid in euros. And in what economists see as an indication of the worsening subprime mortgage crisis, Russia forecloses on Alaska.

On the labor front, the Writers Guild—representing film, television, and radio writers—goes on strike. In solidarity with them, I will not put a punch line here.

The big international story is the Middle East peace conference in Annapolis, Maryland, which is opened by President Bush, who declares that he is "pleased to grant a pardon to this turkey" before being hustled from the room for what aides describe as "a very important meeting." Secretary of State Condoleezza Rice takes over, declaring that the goals of the conference are to "achieve lasting peace between Israelis and Palestinians" and "find a real unicorn." The rest of the conference goes smoothly until what participants describe as a "frank exchange of views" concerning the conference room thermostat setting ends in gunfire.

Abroad, French transit workers attempt to end a strike, only to discover that they have forgotten how to operate the trains. Everybody enjoys a hearty laugh and returns to the café.

As the month draws to a close, Americans celebrate the Thanksgiving holiday much as the early Pilgrims did, lining up outside Best Buy at 3 a.m. to buy steeply discounted appliances.

Speaking of giving thanks, with the end of November comes the end of what has turned out to be another milder-than-usual hurricane season. Hurricane experts, plugging this updated data into their sophisticated computer models, announce that there is "a high statistical probability that next month will be April." This leads us to . . .

DECEMBER

. . . in which the race for the presidency becomes even more riveting than it already was, if such a thing is possible. On the Democratic side, a major spate of snippiness erupts when Barack Obama suggests that Hillary Clinton is more ambitious than he is. In response, Clinton's campaign, showing the wacky sense of humor it is famous for, releases documents showing that Obama thought about running for president when he was in kindergarten. Obama's campaign retaliates by releasing a sonogram allegedly showing that Clinton was running for president in the womb. (I am only making some of this up.)

On the Republican side, Mitt Romney seeks to defuse the religion issue by making a major speech in which—echoing the words of John F. Kennedy—he declares that he is a Catholic. But the big story on the GOP side is former senator or governor of some state Mike (or possibly Bob) Huckabee, who surges ahead in the polls because (a) nobody knows anything about him, and (b) it's fun to say "Huckabee." Huckabee Huckabee Huckabee.

In Washington, President Bush proposes to ease the

subprime-mortgage crisis via a two-pronged program consisting of interest-rate freezes and waterboarding. Outraged congressional Democrats promise to pass a nonbinding resolution containing language so strong that nobody will be able to look directly at it without sunglasses.

In other economic news, retailers report strong holiday sales although shoppers remain wary of Chinese-manufactured toys after a Tennessee Wal-Mart is leveled by what an investigator describes as "the worst Polly Pockets explosion I have ever seen."

Abroad, U.S. intelligence experts release a report stating that Iran is not developing nuclear weapons. This appears to throw a monkey wrench into the Bush administration's Mideast policy, although the president, after aides brief him on a synopsis of the executive summary of the introduction to the report, points out that "it could be referring to a different Iran."

In a major Latin American story, Venezuelan voters reject sweeping constitutional changes pushed by President Hugo Chávez, including a law that would make it illegal for anybody to be taller than he is. A defiant Chávez concedes defeat, but notes that he is still polling ahead of both Joe Biden and John McCain in Iowa.

In sports, a wildly unpredictable season of college football, marked by a slew of upsets, ends with the Bowl Championship Series computer awarding the final number one ranking to Bryn Mawr. The Owls will play the BCS computer's number two ranked team, Vassar, for the 2007 national championship in the Sugar Bowl, scheduled to be played—because of TV marketing requirements—next July.

Meanwhile, NASA suffers yet another black eye when the space shuttle *Vagabond* is launched into orbit carrying a crew of nine, four of whom are discovered, once they get into orbit, to be Hooters waitresses.

But the picture is not so rosy for those of us stuck here on Earth. As we stagger to the end of 2007, we have to face the fact that 2008, being a leap year, will have a whole extra day of alarming events. So as bad as this year was, we should not be in such a hurry to move on. Instead, we should pause for a moment to raise a glass and offer a toast to our friends and loved ones, wishing them health and happiness.

And then we should put the glass down, because it was probably made in China.

AFTERWORD

S o that, dear reader, is where we stand now. I think we can agree, after reading these pages, that the current millennium is off to a bad start. Fortunately, it's early: We still have more than 990 years to go. Things are bound to improve, right?

Hah! If there's one thing we have established in these pages, it's that things always get worse. The serious problems facing us today—terrorism, global warming, war, nuclear proliferation, "reality" television, people walking around wearing cell phone earpieces all the time even when they're not talking on their cell phones—these problems are not going away. At the current rate of decline, this planet could be completely unin-habitable in fifty years.

But does that mean we should all despair? No, it does not. In fact, I am optimistic about the future, and I will tell you why: In fifty years, I plan to be dead. The rest of you are on your own. Good luck, and as you face the future always re-member the words of Abraham Lincoln, or possibly Thomas Edison, who, when asked about the secret of happiness, said something very inspirational, yet, at the same time, very prac-tical. I hope to include it in a later draft of this book.

Among **Dave Barry's** recent bestselling books are his novels *Big Trouble* and *Tricky Business*; the nonfiction *Dave Barry's Money Secrets*; the two Peter Pan prequels, written with Ridley Pearson, *Peter and the Starcatchers* and *Peter and the Shadow Thieves*; and his Christmas story *The Shepherd, the Angel, and Walter the Christmas Miracle Dog*. Barry lives in Coral Gables, Florida. Visit the author's website at www.davebarry.com.